HEALTHY AND AGE-FRIENDLY CITIES IN THE PEOPLE'S REPUBLIC OF CHINA

PROPOSAL FOR HEALTH IMPACT ASSESSMENT AND HEALTHY AND AGE-FRIENDLY CITY ACTION AND MANAGEMENT PLANNING

Najibullah Habib, Stefan Rau, Susann Roth, Filipe Silva, and Janis Shandro

DECEMBER 2020

ASIAN DEVELOPMENT BANK

Contents

Tables, Figures, and Boxes

Acknowledgments

Public health and healthy cities, as well as age-friendly cities and universal design, have been on the agenda of many international agencies, countries, and cities. The authors are grateful to the many experts who prepared and shared materials and lessons on the research, pilot project work, and policies that had been developed. The report is based on the work of many health and urban experts who are creating healthy-city concepts in their roles as city officials, consultants, or officials of international agencies such as the World Health Organization and the Organisation for Economic Co-operation and Development. This report develops an operational framework for a health impact assessment (HIA) and a healthy and age-friendly city action and management plan (HACAMP) that aims to integrate public health into city government and urban planning, and offers conceptual considerations from both health and urban-planning perspectives.

The authors thank James Lynch, M. Teresa Kho, and Sangay Penjor in the East Asia Department of the Asian Development Bank (ADB) for their guidance and support. Thanks also go to fellow author Susann Roth for promoting urban health in ADB since 2013, providing guidance material on HIAs, and proactively supporting the HIA pilot as part of urban-project preparation in ADB's regional departments. The authors are grateful to Wendy Walker for spearheading ADB's early elderly care work in the People's Republic of China (PRC) and for promoting many projects integrating social inclusiveness into urban infrastructure and development projects. She initiated a workshop in 2018, Healthy and Age-Friendly Cities in the PRC, and contributed to this report as a peer reviewer. The authors are grateful for the support of the Health Sector Group, Urban Sector Group, and Social Development Thematic Group of ADB's Sustainable Development and Climate Change Department.

The authors thank Ayumi Konishi, Patrick Osewe, Manoj Sharma, Eduardo Banzon, Eisuke Tajima, Hiroko Uchimura-Shiroishi, Jayati Nigam, Bai Jie, Meredith Wyse, Virinder Sharma, Ma. Victoria Antonio, Okju Jeong, and Francesca Viliani for their comments and suggestions.

The authors are grateful for the inspiration from Belinda Yuen (Singapore) and Wang Lan (Shanghai) who participated in the joint ADB–Tongji University workshop on the topic in 2018.

The authors appreciate the support from government officials in the city of Yanji, Jilin Province, PRC, and the city's Health Bureau, which supported one of the pilots of the HIA, as well as HACAMP for an ADB-financed integrated urban development project. And, last but not least, the authors appreciate the support of the government of the city of Lincang, Yunnan Province, PRC, which assisted with an HIA pilot during the preparation of an ADB-financed project.

Abbreviations

ADB	–	Asian Development Bank
BRT	–	bus rapid transit
CNY	–	Chinese yuan
COVID-19	–	coronavirus disease
GDP	–	gross domestic product
HACAMP	–	healthy and age-friendly city action and management plan
ICT	–	information and communication technology
HIA	–	health impact assessment
HiAP	–	Health in All Policies
km	–	kilometer(s)
NUA	–	New Urban Agenda
OECD	–	Organisation for Economic Co-operation and Development
PRC	–	People's Republic of China
SDG	–	Sustainable Development Goal
UN Habitat	–	United Nations Human Settlements Programme
UNICEF	–	United Nations Children's Fund
Urban HEART	–	Urban Health Equity Assessment and Response Tool
WHO	–	World Health Organization

Executive Summary

This document envisions health and aging issues as opportunities to design better cities in an emerging four-generation urban world. It offers an operational framework aimed at positive outcomes for health and age-friendly, intergenerational cities through integration of urban planning, management, and governance in cross-departmental arrangements and overseen by mayors and other urban leaders. It addresses the key concerns of urban health and age-inclusiveness in cities of various development stages; and it builds on, integrates, and further develops recent research and practice concepts and methods. The framework combines two practical tools for urban planners and city governments: a health impact assessment (HIA) and a healthy and age-friendly city action and management plan (HACAMP) as step-by-step guide. The intended audience includes city governments, managers, planners, and public health professionals, as well as international development agencies such as the Asian Development Bank (ADB). It also includes national or local organizations concerned about human well-being, public health, and urban planning.

These tools are intended to help (i) rehabilitate and/or improve existing cities and urban areas, and (ii) integrate health issues and the needs of an emerging four-generation society into urban master plans and projects. Health and well-being—beyond basic services with clear health outcomes such as water supply, sanitation, and solid waste management—are not traditionally considered drivers of urban development investments, but they can now certainly be considered value additions for urban development investments, especially in high-income and upper-middle-income countries—as for example, the People's Republic of China (PRC). The multitude of existing health issues in urban areas have been exacerbated by the coronavirus disease (COVID-19) pandemic, which further highlights the fact that health and well-being should be drivers of urban rehabilitation, retrofitting, and/or expansion. From the perspective of a multilateral development bank, this would be a welcome change, as health is expected to become more important for city competitiveness, in terms of their ability to attract residents and businesses.

While the initial target country of this report is the PRC, the objectives and framework developed here could also be applied to other countries in Asia and the Pacific and beyond. They are highly relevant for cities at all development stages, especially given the recent pandemic and the demographic transition that has been occurring for some time. Populations around the world have been aging, especially in the high-income and upper-middle-income countries (e.g., the PRC). Life expectancy has increased; birth rates have declined (in the PRC there is also the impact of the one-child policy that was only recently relaxed), resulting in fewer children and smaller households; and work–life patterns are changing, and expected to further transform in various "future-of-work" scenarios. These trends offer opportunities for new forms of community living and elderly-care arrangements, as the sustainability of traditional social-protection systems has been challenged. The scope of priority investments typically depends on the level of development, available infrastructure and services, specific health risks, and demographic profiles.

Most people live in cities. In 2018, the United Nations reported that 55% of the world's population resided in urban areas, a proportion that is expected to increase to 68% by 2050. In the PRC, the urban population has been increasing at an extraordinary high speed, from 17.9% in 1978 to 60.6% at the end of 2019. Urbanization in the PRC has coincided with a demographic transition, with about 20% of the urban population projected to be over 60 years old by 2030; and many of the older people will grow to very advanced ages, becoming part of a four-generation urban society.[1] As the world and the PRC continue to rapidly urbanize, sustainable development will depend on making cities livable, environmentally sustainable, climate resilient, socially and age-inclusive, and competitive. Improvements in the health, well-being, and the quality of life of city residents, both young and old, will contribute to high-quality development in the PRC.

Cities play a pivotal role in health, and the health conditions in urban centers are the focus of much global attention. The World Health Organization (WHO) estimates that 24% of the global health burden stems from urban environments.[2] Human health has played a central role throughout the history of urban planning and in the well-being of urban residents. Life expectancy for urban people in the PRC has increased more than for rural people, and access to health services is better in cities. However, some urban planning paradigms—prioritizing cars over people; situating various urban functions (such as housing, workplaces, commercial centers, and schools) far from each other, and not including sufficient green spaces—have contributed to unhealthy lifestyles and to an increasing burden of noncommunicable diseases. Obesity and road traffic accidents, for example, were exacerbated by car-oriented urban planning. Noncommunicable diseases include cardiovascular disease, diabetes, hypertension, cancer, and respiratory illnesses. Infectious diseases, such as the recent COVID-19 pandemic, spread much faster in dense urban areas.[3] Moreover, the economic and health burden resulting from the focus on economic growth has taken a heavy toll. Health impacts from pollution were estimated to be over $70 billion for half of 2015 alone. Projected economic losses associated with noncommunicable diseases are estimated at $23 trillion for 2012–2030.[4]

Making cities healthier requires multisector urban governance and planning to provide clean and walkable environments, accessible health-care services, and infrastructure that improves the urban environment, as all of these will ease public health management

---

[1]   United Nations. 2018. *The World's Cities in 2018: Data Booklet.* New York.

[2]   A. Prüss-Üstün et al. 2016. *Preventing Disease through Healthy Environments: A Global Assessment of the Burden of Disease from Environmental Risks.* Geneva: WHO.

[3]   Some may argue that prevention of future infectious outbreaks will require low-density urban development. Two aspects are important to consider: (i) governments can reduce and manage outbreaks in urban areas, as they have done in the Republic of Korea, the PRC, and in some European and other countries; and (ii) infectious diseases will likely spread during limited periods, so the sacrifice of other compelling social, environmental, and economic benefits would need to be carefully weighed against the possible benefits of alternative development models that emphasize temporary epidemics and pandemics. Certainly, linkages such as those between waterborne diseases and polluted water, pulmonary diseases and polluted air, and stress and too much noise or insufficient green spaces, are factors that must be taken into account.

[4]   These estimates were prepared prior to the COVID-19 pandemic, so they do not consider economic losses caused by the pandemic and by the responses to it.

in an era when infectious diseases, noncommunicable diseases, and the challenges of increasingly aging populations are converging, as in the case of the PRC. Well-integrated, best-practice urban planning and urban design is already creating positive health co-benefits and, if further improved, they could turn cities into vehicles for preventing primary diseases and improving health outcomes. For example, the development of mixed-use pedestrian-friendly areas, served by safe and convenient public transport, attractive public spaces and green parks, sports facilities, and public toilet facilities can help improve air and surface water quality, urban microclimate, fitness facilities, and social connections that promote physical and mental health. Well-planned decentralized and conveniently located urban health services ideally within walking distance to many residents and public transport, early detection of infectious diseases, and measures for vulnerable groups such as the elderly can help reduce noncommunicable diseases, help control infectious diseases, and promote well-being.

Urban health investments can effectively and efficiently benefit a growing urban and aging population. Cities must, therefore, govern, plan, and invest holistically in the promotion of public and community health, healthy lifestyles, gender and age equality, disease prevention, and improved social services. This effort needs to be integrated with universal urban design to ensure that public spaces, sidewalks, parks, and buildings are accessible for people of all ages and the physically impaired. Cities need to integrate an age-friendly public transport system with safe and convenient sidewalks, bicycle parking, parks, public spaces, and public service facilities. The much needed low-carbon, climate-resilient urban planning and design would also contribute to improved health benefits from reduced emissions and the reduced risk of climate-related disasters such as flooding, droughts, heat waves, and storm surges, which also endanger lives and safety. City initiatives can be highly effective in implementing health sector interventions. For example, tobacco regulations are successfully implemented with rigor at the city level, including in Beijing; and in the city of Luzhou, in Sichuan Province, the local government offers free physical examinations to all its residents.

The authors propose an operational framework that is applicable to both existing urban areas and proposed urban master plans for new areas and projects, builds on city health sector plans, fits within the context of sector operations and plans, and contributes to urban master development plans and local institutional arrangements and responsibilities. This framework is based on a two-stage, holistic, and evidence-based approach: (i) the conduct of an HIA,[5] to be further developed to analyze and manage urban health risks, impacts, and opportunities; and (ii) the preparation, adoption, and implementation of a HACAMP. The HIA and HACAMP will be developed by interdisciplinary teams including health specialists, city planners, environment specialists, and others, in close cooperation with local government departments, and considering and benefiting all citizens, including children, the elderly, and the physically and mentally impaired.

The HIA and HACAMP will aim to control communicable diseases and significantly prevent and reduce contemporary noncommunicable diseases, including mental illnesses, and to promote healthy lifestyles. The HACAMP will include actions to improve (i) environmental

---

[5]   ADB. 2018. *Health Impact Assessment: A Good Practice Sourcebook*. Manila. The HIA will be a combination of procedures, methods, and tools that systematically evaluate the potential effects of a policy, plan, program, or project on the health of a population and the distribution of those effects within the population. The HIA will also identify actions to manage those effects.

health factors (air, water, soil quality, and noise levels, among others); (ii) basic urban services associated with health (access to safe water supplies; sanitation; hygiene; solid waste management, including adequate medical waste management, which is especially important for infectious disease medical waste,[6] and sufficient social and affordable housing); (iii) specific health-care services and access to them (general practitioners, community health centers, hospitals, specialty hospitals, various forms of elderly care, ambulance systems, and access to health insurance, among others); (iv) urban actions that enable healthier and safer lifestyles (a dense, pleasant, and safe network of pedestrian and bicycle paths; convenient and safe public transport; public green spaces; public and private sports areas and exercise equipment; smoke- and alcohol-free areas); (v) urban and building design features such as the accessibility of public spaces and facilities and public transport for people of all ages; and (vi) programs and financing at the city and national levels to promote human capital development in the health and elderly care service sectors, considering the significant shortages in health and elderly care workers and the regional and urban–rural disparities in the distribution and capacity of such workers in the PRC and many other countries.

The HIA and HACAMP aim to advance urban livability, well-being, and people-centered urban planning and management, which will ensure improved health outcomes and benefits, contributing to the PRC's Healthy China 2030 program and aligning with other urban policies and programs.[7] Expected impacts are healthier people who enjoy a higher life expectancy, and increased productivity and quality of life in more livable cities that are greener, cleaner, and safer. Healthy and age-friendly cities are well served by public transport; feature an attractive pedestrian and cycling environment; have accessible, safe, and convenient urban spaces, services, and amenities; benefit from improved urban governance; and are made safer due to higher disaster risk preparedness and response capacity.[8] The HIA and HACAMP align with various Sustainable Development Goals (SDGs), especially with goal 3 (to ensure healthy lives and promote well-being for all at all ages), and with ADB Strategy 2030, especially operational priority 4 (making cities more livable).[9]

The HIA will evaluate health- and age-associated risks, impact, and opportunities in existing urban areas and new urban master plans or projects, map out structural and nonstructural options to mitigate risk and leverage health benefits, and ensure that healthy and age-friendly design-making is built into all urban development. The HIA will lay out options for mitigating risk and improving health, including stringently monitoring health outcomes and prioritizing interventions. HIA outputs will include the following:

(i)   the establishment of an urban health team comprising public health and medical experts, planners, and various experts and officials across administrative departments to enable interdisciplinary assessment and action; coordination of

---

[6]   ADB. 2020. *Managing Infectious Medical Waste during the COVID-19 Pandemic.* Manila. ADB is providing technical support and provided guidelines for handling COVID-19 medical waste and infectious waste.

[7]   Government of the People's Republic of China, Central Committee of the Chinese Communist Party and the State Council of the People's Republic of China. 2016. *The Plan for "Healthy China 2030."* Beijing.

[8]   The HIA and HACAMP will be developed analogously to environmental impact assessments and environmental management plans, which serve to operationalize environmental safeguards in ADB project preparation, implementation, and post-project monitoring and evaluation.

[9]   ADB. 2019. *Strategy 2030: Operational Plan for Priority 4: Making Cities More Livable, 2019–2024.* Manila.

work plans; and a review of existing national and local health sector plans, roles, responsibilities, and associated budgets;

(ii)   a health- and age-focused risk assessment of an existing urban area, with a registry and maps that highlight and prioritize urban risks to health, considering children, women, the elderly, and persons with disabilities; and options, including structural and nonstructural improvements, assessment of the health and elderly care sector workforce ratio to the city's population, and an assessment of spatial distribution efficiency and accessibility, as well as institutional, economic, and financial efficiency;

(iii)   an assessment of opportunities to improve health and promote healthy lifestyles in planned new urban projects, and of how the projects would improve urban areas and contribute to improvements in service delivery efficiency;

(iv)   an assessment of potential health impacts of urban and district master plans, urban design plans, and of inputs to health-proof them; and

(v)   mapping of options for structural and nonstructural health-risk-mitigation measures, and an assessment of these options, including preliminary comparative economic analysis that will rank options by optimizing costs and benefits.

The HACAMP will identify the most impactful structural and nonstructural measures and lay out a prioritized action and investment plan to optimize health and well-being. It will build on the results of the HIA; prioritize actions and investments; identify roles and responsibilities, financial and human-resource requirements; and develop an implementation schedule to improve health outcomes. The HACAMP will retrofit plans for existing urban areas and proposals for new projects or urban expansion initiatives; and these plans will include structural and nonstructural elements. It will feed into feasibility studies, scoping exercises, baseline information, business cases, and the strategic frameworks of the master plan to include high quality of living. HACAMP outputs will include the following:

(i)   for existing urban areas, a retrofitting plan that outlines actions, roles and responsibilities, financial and human-resource requirements, investment prioritization, and an implementation schedule for structural and nonstructural measures to comprehensively improve health aspects, with special consideration for children, the elderly, and the physically impaired;

(ii)   for new urban project proposals, inclusion of health management plans and complementary structural and nonstructural investments to ensure healthy and age-friendly design, such as application of universal design principles to ensure that public spaces, facilities, and transport contribute to residents' well-being, and that the needs of the elderly and persons with disabilities are considered;

(iii)   for urban and district master plans and urban design, a "health-proofing" review and increased health and elderly care service-delivery efficiency to fully integrate healthy and age-friendly urban aspects and ensure that health is safeguarded on all levels and sectors and promoted during planning and implementation;

(iv)   a management plan covering governance, implementation arrangements and schedules, roles and responsibilities, and financing and budget plans, while taking efficiency into account; and

(v)   an urban health monitoring and evaluation plan, including special consideration for children, the elderly, and the physically impaired.

1 Health and Aging as Opportunities in an Urbanizing Four-Generation World

There is an urgent need for health impact assessments (HIAs) and healthy and age-friendly city action and management plans (HACAMPs). Health and well-being in cities will be central for people and communities and an essential factor for cities' competitiveness, especially in a post–coronavirus disease (COVID-19) world. Urban centers became the central focus of the pandemic as overcrowding, hot spots, and bad air quality exacerbated people's vulnerability to the infection. Urban health and aging are closely linked, as the share of older people increases in cities, requiring changes in policies and public health perspectives. Urbanization challenges include continued social and demographic inclusion, community cohesion, social-protection systems and urban fiscal sustainability (both facing significant systemic challenges), and environmental and climate change. Many countries, cities, and communities are evolving into four-generation urban societies characterized by small families, small households, and single-person households; with more elderly, and many them reaching high age, and fewer babies, children, and young adults. This four-generation social structure will require a more vibrant and interconnected community life. The future of work and technology will likely lead to a polarization of work and employment, with more people retreating into precarious and informal employment arrangements, changing their work-life patterns, or advancing toward technology opportunities such as those found in age-friendly smart cities and communities.

People are becoming urbanites and living longer. Urbanization is a key determinant of health and welfare across the globe and, by 2050, about 68% of humans will live in urban areas, as Africa and Asia will have caught up rapidly with other regions.[10] In the People's Republic of China (PRC), the urban population increased from 17.9% in 1978 to 59.2% in 2018, and is expected to reach 70% in 2030.[11] The number of people aged 60 and older will represent 18%–20% of the total PRC population by 2030.[12] The aged population is expected to reach 437 million in 2051, when one out of three Chinese will be aged 60 and older, and people aged 80 and older will rise to 90 million.[13] The process of urbanization coincides with an increase of life expectancy overall. Urban women in the PRC lived on

---

[10] United Nations, Department of Economic and Social Affairs. News: 68% of the World Population Project to Live in Urban Areas by 2050, Says UN.

[11] United Nations Department of Economic and Social Affairs, Population Division. 2019. *World Urbanization Prospects: The 2018 Revision*. New York.

[12] Q. Chen, E. Dietzenbacher, and B. Los. The Effects of Ageing and Urbanisation on China's Future Rural and Urban Populations. 2017. *Asian Population Studies*. 13 (2). pp. 172–197; Y. Zeng and T. Hesketh. 2016. The Effects of China's Universal Two-Child Policy. *Lancet*. 388 (10054). pp. 1930–1938.

[13] *People's Daily*. 2006. China's Elderly Population Reaches 143 million. 13 May; Y. Wang, E. Gonzales, and N. Morrow-Howell. 2017. Applying WHO's Age-Friendly Communities Framework to a National Survey in China. *Journal of Gerontological Social Work*. 60 (3). pp. 215–231.

average 6.64 years longer than rural women in 2010, and urban men lived on average 7.09 years longer than rural men.[14]

Cities can place a heavy burden on environmental and health issues. The PRC has achieved remarkable progress since its opening up and reform policies started in 1978. Industrialization and urbanization lifted millions out of poverty, and urban infrastructure and assets have been built at an unprecedented rate. Despite the positive impacts on infrastructure, services, disposable incomes, and life expectancy, the negative impacts on the urban environment and health are significant, and the financial and health burden resulting from a focus on economic growth has taken a heavy toll. Health impacts from pollution were estimated to be over \$70 billion for half of 2015 alone.[15] Projected economic losses associated with noncommunicable diseases, including cardiovascular disease, diabetes, cancer, and respiratory illnesses, are estimated to be \$23 trillion from 2012 to 2030.[16] Urban centers have a higher prevalence of noncommunicable disease than rural centers. At the same time, densely populated cities can become centers of outbreaks and epidemics—as in the case of Wuhan, a city of more than 11 million people, where COVID-19 started and spread widely—via centralized hospital systems and among infected people who had come in close contact with the uninfected. Human density in cities, and the connectivity of cities by land, water, and air lead to the easy spread of infectious diseases beyond the cities and national borders. The spread is particularly difficult to manage if new emerging infectious diseases come into play. However, such situations tend to have time limits, while cities and urban areas provide a long-lasting physical framework for organizing human life, and even some wildlife. Therefore, whether or not such urban areas should be altered must be considered from a long-term perspective that takes into account all the social, environmental, economic, and cultural benefits that well-planned urban areas generate because of their density; mix of uses; sustainable mobility options, including mass public transit; and green space systems.[17]

Continued urban development needs to integrate health and aging aspects. As the PRC moves from an approach to development focused on gross domestic product (GDP) increase to one focused on quality (social inclusion and environment improvements and others) in its 13th Five-Year Plan for Economic and Social Development,[18] continued rapid urbanization presents both challenges and opportunities, and integrating health issues becomes critical. Integrated and sustainable urban and regional planning, governance, and management require coordination, environmental management, adequate urban infrastructure and services, good-quality housing, sustainable urban transport, water supply and sanitation, solid waste management, drainage and flood-risk management, energy supply, health care (converging disease profiles, aging populations), education, and

Many countries, cities, and communities are evolving into four-generation urban societies characterized by small families, small households, and single-person households; with more elderly, and many them reaching high-ages, and fewer babies, children, and young adults.

---

[14]   J. Yang et al. 2018. The Tsinghua-Lancet Commission on Healthy Cities in China: Unlocking the Power of Cities for a Healthy China. *Lancet*. 391 (10135). pp. 2140–2184.

[15]   H. Wang et al. 2016. Global, Regional, and National Life Expectancy, All-Cause Mortality, and Cause-Specific Mortality for 249 Causes of Death, 1980–2015: A Systematic Analysis for the Global Burden of Disease Study 2015. *Lancet*. 388 (10053). pp. 1459–1544.

[16]   D.E. Bloom et al. 2014. The Macroeconomic Impact of Non-Communicable Diseases in China and India: Estimates, Projections, and Comparisons. *Journal of the Economics of Ageing*. 4. pp. 100–111.

[17]   For principles recommended for the PRC, for example, see: S. Rau. 2018. Eco-Cities in Europe: Compact, Mixed-use, Green, Livable New Districts. In L. Wang and S. Rau, eds. *New Towns and New Districts Case Studies from the People's Republic of China*. Manila and Shanghai: ADB and Tongji University, College of Architecture and Urban Planning.

[18]   Central Committee of the Communist Party of China. 2016. *The 13th Five-Year Plan for Economic and Social Development of the People's Republic of China (2016–2020)*. Beijing.

employment. The emergence of a four-generation urban society is a significant societal shift that requires city policy review and adjustments—specifically, in how urban communities live together and how social services are organized and financed with health and well-being at the center of sustainable development of cities, regardless of size and development stage. The PRC is a unique case for several reasons: its deeply rooted culture of healthy lifestyles; vibrant community life; increased life expectancies; the migration of the working-age population from rural areas to major urban centers; and the demographic transition caused by the one-child policy from 1980 to 2016, and now by the two-child policy. An important consideration in integrating health and aging into urban planning and management is the long-term demographic transition and resulting population decline, including many cities. The population is expected to be reduced by half by 2100, starting at mid-century, with one-third of all urban areas in the PRC already seeing declining populations from out-migration, mostly smaller provincial cities.[19]

Innovative approaches to healthy and age-friendly cities are necessary. Many of the present approaches to urban planning and city building do not meet the needs and challenges of the rapidly growing urban population, who must remain healthy and have a high quality of life to be economically productive. City planners and public health officials rarely have meaningful exchanges on the best ways to plan healthy cities. This report describes how related disciplines—urban planning and public health management—can come together to develop healthy and age-friendly cities based on a flexible HIA and a HACAMP framework.

Healthy and age-friendly cities align with sustainable development. Leveraging healthy and age-friendly cities to become an integral part of environmentally sustainable, socially inclusive, and economically competitive urban development is critical. In developed countries, where basic services have been met and life expectancies extended, the challenges may lie in promoting healthy lifestyles and healthy communities. Cities in developing countries have to ensure that fundamental risks to health are mitigated, by ensuring clean air, surface water, and soil; acceptable noise levels; and other environmental factors; as well as safe drinking water and sanitation, food, clothing and shelter, solid waste management, education, and basic health services.

Application of HIA and HACAMP in urban projects can influence urban investment decisions. The question of whether health and age-friendly considerations could be drivers for urban investments needs to be discussed—including such factors as the development stage and other particular circumstances—to determine the nature of the applications of an HIA and HACAMP. For example, many urban infrastructure programs and projects in the PRC, including many financed by multilateral development agencies, directly contribute to positive public health outcomes by providing access to safe water and sanitation, solid waste management, and reducing flood risk, among other benefits. Under such projects, the HIA and HACAMP would focus on strengthening the positive outcomes of the planned investments, providing systematic sector assessment, and on planning for the addition of further health and age-friendly benefits that align with the general objectives of the project.

---

[19]   For a more detailed description of the challenges in addressing long-term demographic challenges and integrating medium-term needs, please see: S. Rau. Forthcoming 2020. *Strategic Policy Options for Urbanization in the People's Republic of China. East Asia Working Paper Series.* Manila: ADB.

The HIA and HACAMP could also be seen as an additional dimension and added value to urban development and/or infrastructure projects (both domestic or externally financed). In such cases, there would be additional incremental investments leading to further health and age-friendly benefits. Then incremental costs would have to be compared against economic benefits. In the case study of Yanji (Chapter 8), the additional incremental investments are fairly small compared with the anticipated benefits for urban livability and more conscious living of the residents (through consultations and awareness raising), with more physical activity and more green spaces, and better urban microclimates, air quality, and exercise equipment (bicycle, pedestrian, and jogging paths; public toilets; smoke- and alcohol-free zones). The authors believe that HIA and HACAMP should be considered and mainstreamed as constructive tools, as they present a valuable opportunity to generate some additional health benefits, given that they align with or create many co-benefits for low-carbon, climate-resilient, sustainable urban development. Moreover, the incremental costs are quite low compared with the multiple benefits (including health) created.

Health, safety, and well-being can be drivers of new types of urban projects. In the context of the PRC's Healthy China 2030 strategy, launched in 2016 (following the Hygienic City Campaign, operational since 1992), and from the perspective of a multilateral regional development bank, the authors strongly recommend that health, safety, and well-being be given a more central role when considering urban development support. The authors also believe that urban projects can be driven by the health and age-friendly needs of people (including children in a four-generation urban world), and that these projects could become an integral part of a people-centered approach to urban development, especially urban rehabilitation and retrofitting. This would contribute to the overall objective of livable cities through the integration of these dimensions into planning and management. An HIA and HACAMP will contribute to more inclusive development, and likely to greener and more environmentally sustainable development (through additional, better-designed green spaces and healthier lifestyle options, as in the Yanji case). They will also likely result in more economically competitive development, as cities will become more attractive, with features that can be marketed to attract and retain qualified workers, companies, and jobs.

In the context of COVID-19, all these considerations have even greater relevance, as people have become more concerned about sound health service systems and healthy lifestyle options in an urban environment. Hence, the authors are hopeful that in the case of the PRC as an upper-middle-income country, a focus on health and elderly care, and on their integration into urban development, may serve as a starting point for some projects. If that occurs, these projects should provide lessons for other developing member countries of the Asian Development Bank (ADB), lessons that go beyond the goal of adding value to urban infrastructure and services; and these lessons should be mainstreamed, as mentioned above. For the PRC, this starting point could also fulfill a significant task for the medium- and long-term future: the rehabilitation and retrofitting of existing cities and urban areas, including many urban districts built since the 1980s that lack livability and options for healthy lifestyles. As an example, in some major developed cities, obesity has become a serious health problem for many residents, one that is directly related to lifestyles and urban planning. Features such as suburban development with wide roads and no sidewalks in residential neighborhoods, and long distances to schools, shops, and parks, are very conducive to driving, but less so to walking or cycling. Some mayors have been making it their key mission to fight obesity, and they have been successful through urban transformation and awareness-raising campaigns that gave rise to lifestyle changes.

Human capital development can address shortages in health and elderly care sectors. The global shortage of health-care workers will reach more than 15 million by 2030. Many countries face a substantial and widening mismatch between the demand, expressed in the required numbers of health-care workers, and supply, expressed in a country's capacity to educate, train, and employ them. Health and elderly care needs will become more complex due to aging and to the increasing number of people with noncommunicable diseases and chronic illnesses, and there will be a stronger demand for nursing care services and home-visit care among the elderly. To achieve universal health coverage, health systems in all countries require an adequate number of trained health professionals providing quality care. In the PRC, the deficit of health professionals is alarming, with three nurses per 1,000 population, which is far below the average for member countries of the Organisation for Economic Co-operation and Development (OECD) of around nine nurses per 1,000 population.

Many countries face a substantial and widening mismatch between the demand, expressed in the required numbers of health-care workers, and supply, expressed in a country's capacity to educate, train, and employ them.

2 "Healthy Cities," "Age-Friendly Cities," and "Child-Friendly Cities" Concepts and Programs

The concept of healthy and age-friendly cities aims at the integration of previously isolated concepts. Its purpose is to contribute to an overall objective of making cities more livable and, in the case of ADB operations, to contribute to ADB's Strategy 2030 and its operational plans, including the Operational Plan for Priority 4: Making Cities More Livable.[20] This integrative concept builds on a wealth of work—by the World Health Organization (WHO), United Nations Human Settlements Programme (UN Habitat), United Nations Children's Fund (UNICEF), and many other organizations and municipal governments. These concepts and initiatives in urban planning, urban design, urban management, and governance remain highly relevant: they target urban health, the needs of elderly people and the issues surrounding aging in cities, and/or child-responsive or family-friendly city planning. The proposed HIA and HACAMP framework seeks to promote and achieve the integration of these areas and to expand into more detailed concepts regarding the new opportunities presented by community life in cities with four generations under one roof, including more elderly people and fewer children, smaller families or patchwork families, and more single households. It is expected to highlight the many overlapping considerations and co-benefits of proposed structural and nonstructural measures from the various approaches. The further integration of state-of-the-art urban planning and design concepts—such as low-carbon, climate-resilient cities and eco-cities—will deliver a wide range of co-benefits for health and aging in place, and for intergenerational community life.

There should be a holistic concept of health. According to WHO, health is not merely the absence of disease, but a state of complete physical, mental, and social well-being,[21] as well as a resource for living a full life. To reach such a state of well-being, people must be able to identify and realize their aspirations, satisfy their needs, and change or cope with their environment. Health is, therefore, a resource for everyday life, not simply the objective of living. Health is a positive concept emphasizing social and personal resources, as well as physical capacities.[22]

The health aspects of city planning date back to antiquity. Health has played a central role in the history of urban development. Early city planners considered health promotion and protection, sustainable development, and ecological balance when locating new settlements and cities and arranging and linking the various functions in cities.[23] Ancient Rome had a

---

[20]   ADB. 2019. *Strategy 2030: Operational Plan for Priority 4*; ADB. 2019. *Strategy 2030 Operational Plans Overview*. Manila.

[21]   WHO. 1946. Preamble to the Constitution of WHO. Adopted by the International Health Conference. New York. 19 June–22 July.

[22]   WHO. 1986. *The Ottawa Charter for Health Promotion*. Adopted at the First International Conference on Health Promotion. Ottawa. 21 November.

[23]   L.J. Duhl and A.K. Sanchez. 1999. *Healthy Cities and the City Planning Process: A Background Document on Links between Health and Urban Planning*. Copenhagen: WHO Regional Office for Europe; E. de Leeuw and J. Simos, eds. 2017. *Healthy Cities: The Theory, Policy, and Practice of Value-Based Urban Planning*. New York: Springer-Verlag.

number of water sources and an elaborate water-supply infrastructure, including aqueducts; they also had sewers, public latrines, and bathhouses. Cities in Europe suffered plague and cholera epidemics during the Middle Ages. In response, they had hygiene rules and land-use regulations, and they managed activities like animal markets, which in many cases were held outside the city walls. Hospitals were often built outside the city walls to prevent contagion from entering the city, and quarantine measures were first introduced in cities to help prevent the spread of diseases from incoming foreign vehicles or vessels.

In the 19th century, when Europe and the United States were undergoing a period of rapid industrialization and urbanization, city planners took into account discoveries of the causes of waterborne and airborne diseases (e.g., contaminated water and untreated sewage), so they invested in sewer systems and sanitation. London was one of the many cities where this occurred. City planners also integrated water-supply and sanitation infrastructure and improved hygienic conditions as part of their massive urban expansion plans.[24] Critiques of urban conditions, especially the congested worker housing and pollution from factories, led to the concept of garden cities served by commuter rail in England, and to urban parks inside cities in many European and North American cities, one example being New York City's Central Park (which was initiated through a civic society movement). These critiques also led to the concept of separating land uses—for instance, locating industrial zones away from residential areas—which influenced modernist planners in the 1920s and has been widely applied to this day. Now, the positive benefits of urban green space systems for health, healthy lifestyles, social inclusion, clean air, carbon sequestration, microclimates, water filtration, stormwater retention, and other needs and functions are well known, and are routinely included in state-of-the-art concepts and plans.[25]

According to WHO, health is not merely the absence of disease, but a state of complete physical, mental, and social well-being, as well as a resource for living a full life.

Ancient water infrastructure. On the left is the famous Pont du Gard, an ancient Roman aqueduct in southern France (photo by Natalie Azarova); and on the right is an ancient sewer in Cologne, Germany, which was founded by the Romans in the 1st century AD (photo from Xanara, Wikicommons).

[24]   P. Hall. 1996. *Cities of Tomorrow: An Intellectual History of Urban Planning and Design in the Twentieth Century* (updated edition). Oxford, United Kingdom: Blackwell.

[25]   WHO Regional Office for Europe. 2017. *Urban Green Spaces: A Brief for Action.* Copenhagen.

The United Nations New Urban Agenda (NUA) and Sustainable Development Goals (SDGs) both recognize that health is not only desirable, but also a prerequisite and fundamental driver of sustainable development and urban development. Urbanization remains one of the 21st century's most transformative trends; the NUA was adopted at the United Nations Conference on Housing and Sustainable Urban Development (Habitat III), in 2016. The NUA tackles the challenges and opportunities associated with ever-increasing urbanization, referencing the 2030 Agenda for Sustainable Development and its 17 SDGs, the Paris Agreement on low-carbon development, and all the other recent relevant global development agreements and frameworks. The NUA is based on a list of shared principles, with the overarching commitment to not leave anyone behind, promote development that is people-centered, protect the planet, and help realize all human rights and fundamental freedoms. The NUA presents the fundamental standards and principles for planning, constructing, developing, managing, and improving urban areas based on five pillars: national urban policies, urban legislation and regulations, urban planning and design, local economy and municipal finance, and local implementation. Urbanization should be an "engine of sustained and inclusive economic growth, social and cultural development, and environmental protection." To "improve human health and well-being" is a key objective of the NUA.[26]

Healthy-city programs have been implemented since the 1980s. As we become an urban species, cities and metropolitan areas must provide for the health and well-being of people of all ages in a holistic way. Policy makers around the world agree that placing people first and making cities livable are the most important considerations in new urban developments and in existing cities. Healthy cities have become a key goal in many countries. Since the 1980s, WHO has cooperated on developing healthy cities in various countries. The PRC has been carrying out a Hygienic City Campaign since 1990, and in 2016 adopted the Healthy China 2030 program, of which healthy cities are a key component. WHO's description of its healthy cities concept is presented in Box 1. Healthy and age-friendly cities are aligned with, and contribute to, the overarching objective of livable cities, which encompasses a broader set of factors than are generally associated with a high quality of life.[27]

Healthy and age-friendly cities should have a list of priorities similar to a hierarchy of needs. The first priority of a healthy city is the provision of the basic needs of life, such as food, water, sanitation, and shelter; the next priorities should be the attainment of a better quality of life and the achievement of personal aspirations. Healthy cities should follow a priority action plan that is comparable to Abraham Maslow's pyramid of needs, translated from the individual to the level of a city (Figure 1). Viewing cities and urban planning through the lens of a health-needs hierarchy unveils a framework of planning and design through which we can evaluate existing urban areas and propose new urban development that is holistically responsive to human health. Healthy cities should first ensure that basic health needs are met (i.e., physiological needs and safety, and the elimination or reduction of exposure to infectious diseases). Then, healthy lifestyles and healthy communities should be promoted, and the risks of noncommunicable diseases such as cardiovascular diseases and cancer should be reduced, resulting in longer life expectancies. Healthy cities should enable a high quality of living; heathy lifestyle choices that are easy to make; and the self-fulfillment

---

[26]   United Nations Conference on Housing and Sustainable Urban Development. 2017. *New Urban Agenda*. New York: United Nations. p. 3.

[27]   The Economist Intelligence Unit. The Global Livability Index (accessed 22 Sept 2020). The Economic Intelligence Unit assigns a score for over 30 qualitative and quantitative factors across the six broad categories of stability, health care, culture, environment, education, and infrastructure.

of citizens, families, and communities. The planning of healthy cities should consider all aspects of physical and mental health, vibrant and diverse human interactions, and culture and education to ensure that all urban residents can develop to their full potential.

Cities play a pivotal role in development and economic growth, and their health conditions are the focus of much global attention. WHO estimates that 24% of the global health burden stems from urban environments.[28] Recent literature reviews identify neighborhood design, housing, food environments, natural and sustainable environments, and transport as key determinants of healthy urban settings.[29]

Figure 1: A Hierarchy of Urban Health and Well-Being

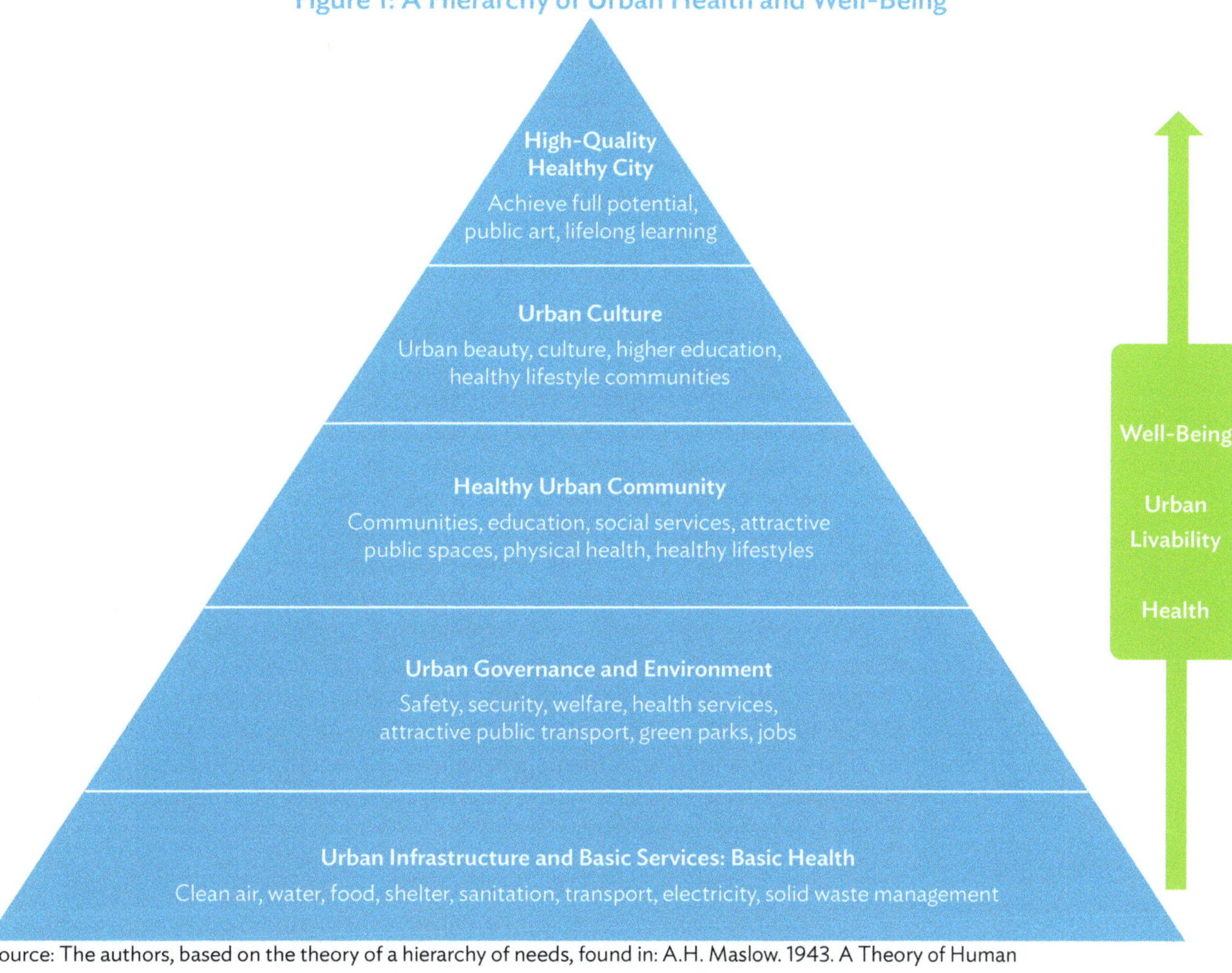

Source: The authors, based on the theory of a hierarchy of needs, found in: A.H. Maslow. 1943. A Theory of Human Motivation. *Psychological Review.* 50 (4). pp. 370–396.

[28]   S. Su et al. 2016. Public Health in Linkage to Land Use: Theoretical Framework, Empirical Evidence, and Critical Implications for Reconnecting Health Promotion to Land Use Policy. *Land Use Policy.* 57. pp. 605–618.

[29]   E. Bird et al. 2017. *Healthy People Healthy Places Evidence Tool: Evidence and Practical Linkage for Design, Planning and Health.* Technical Report. Bristol: University of the West of England; M. Davern et al. 2017. *Quality Green Space Supporting Health, Wellbeing and Biodiversity: A Literature Review.* Report prepared for the National Heart Foundation of Australian (South Australian Division); Government of South Australia, Department of Environment, Water and Natural Resources and the Office for Recreation and Sport; South Australian Local Government Association; and the University of Melbourne. Adelaide: The National Heart Foundation of Australia (South Australian Division).

Age-friendly cities. WHO's work on age-friendly cities identifies key urban sectors that influence the health of urban residents, such as transport, housing, employment, health and social care services, and parks and other green spaces.[30] Social participation, respect and social inclusion, civic participation, communication and information, and community support are also highlighted as key urban health issues. Universal design features, the ability to modify and maintain one's home, housing options, and living environments that are safe and secure and provide privacy are important features of age-friendly buildings and outdoor spaces.

The specific attributes of streets, shops, greenways, parks, and public transportation stations are important for providing active and healthy aging. A significant amount of work has focused on the physical health aspects (preventive care, functioning and disabilities, injuries, perceived health, hypertension, arthritis symptoms, mortality) of aging in the built environment.[31] Applying WHO's age-friendly communities framework to the PRC context highlights additional important aspects, including the ability to meet basic needs, migration, and the availability of welfare benefits and support.[32] Research on Asian populations has confirmed the importance of personal, social, and environmental factors—including exercise, access to walking aids, and continued connection to people in one's community—as essential for physical and mental well-being and a high quality of life.[33]

Recent urban development in the PRC has offered positive health opportunities, including access to improved health services. Urban residents have a longer life expectancy than their rural counterparts.[34] A number of challenges in the PRC's urban centers have health implications, as outlined by the Tsinghua–Lancet Commission on Healthy Cities in China (Figure 2). These include air and water pollution, the emergence of noncommunicable diseases, consistent internal migration to support continued economic growth, lifestyle changes, inconvenient public and nonmotorized transport options, extreme climate events, and changes in social equity. The commission emphasizes how to adapt to a changing urban population that is increasingly aged, and with disabilities (footnote 14). Negative health outcomes associated with these challenges include cardiovascular diseases, diabetes, cancer, respiratory illnesses, mental disorders, and injuries, along with emerging infectious and communicable diseases (footnote 30). Additional pressures from disasters and lack of resilience to climate change-related events must also be acknowledged. In this context of risks and opportunities, the urban planning imperative must be to improve population health and lower health-care costs, while boosting productivity and urban competitiveness as mutually reinforcing co-benefits.

---

[30]   WHO. 2007. *Global Age-Friendly Cities: A Guide.* Geneva.

[31]   M.J. Koohsari, T. Nakaya, and K. Oka. 2018. Activity-Friendly Built Environments in a Super-Aged Society, Japan: Current Challenges and toward a Research Agenda. *International Journal of Environmental Research and Public Health.* 2018; 15(9):2054. Published 19 September 2018. doi: 10.3390/ijerph15092054; N. Garin et al. 2014. Built Environment and Elderly Population Health: A Comprehensive Literature Review. *Clinical Practice & Epidemiology in Mental Health.* 10. pp. 103–115.

[32]   Y. Wang, E. Gonzales, and N. Morrow-Howell, 2017. Applying WHO's Age-Friendly Communities Framework to a National Survey in China. *Journal of Gerontological Social Work.* 60 (3). pp. 215–231.

[33]   J. Kerr, D. Rosenberg, and L. Frank. 2012. The Role of the Built Environment in Healthy Aging: Community Design, Physical Activity, and Health among Older Adults. *Journal of Planning Literature.* 27 (1). pp. 43–60.

[34]   G. Yang and S. Liu. 2015. Analysis on the Average Life Expectancy in Population of China Based on Bayesian Random-Effect Model. *Statistical Research.* 32. pp. 95–100.

Generations living together. New concepts of multigenerational housing in Sweden demonstrate the possibility of vibrant community life and new friendships between younger and older adults living as singles in a housing block with shared spaces (photo by the British Broadcasting Corporation).

Child-friendly cities. With regard to child-friendly cities, UNICEF's guidelines on child-responsive urban planning conclude that many urban settings are not safe or sustainable. The guidelines call for cities where children can live in healthy, safe, inclusive, green, and prosperous communities.[35] Access to services and education will be other domains with important opportunities for children. The Bernard van Leer Foundation takes the perspective of an average 3-year-old as a basis for adjusting the urban realm.[36]

UNICEF calls for prioritizing children in urban planning in three dimensions: (i) area-based: planning urban spaces at various scales to enable better service delivery for children, as well as a clean and safe built environment; (ii) process-based: engaging children and other local stakeholders in building partnerships to produce child-responsive cities; and (iii) evidence-based: using geographic and socioeconomic urban data platforms to consider spatial inequity, and identifying areas and dimensions in which children are disadvantaged.

The urgency of child-inclusive cities is most evident in developing countries, where the total global number of slum dwellers grew to 880 million—about 300 million of them children. They suffer particularly from unhealthy and unsafe living conditions, and are most vulnerable to inadequate housing, unsanitary conditions, and inadequate infrastructure and

---

35   UNICEF. 2018. *Shaping Urbanization for Children: A Handbook on Child-Responsive Urban Planning.* New York.

36   Bernard van Leer Foundation. 2019. *An Urban95 Starter Kit: Ideas for Action.* The Hague, Netherlands.

services. Unplanned, fragmented, informal sprawling developments are common patterns of development, and the lack of planning for education, health, and basic services affect children who have limited options for childcare, education, interactions with other children, and playgrounds. In fact, many children have to struggle to support the family income in the informal economy. In upper-middle-income and high-income countries, children are typically raised in small families or by single parents, most lack integration into a functioning community, and many lack relationships with their grandparents and with older and elderly people in general. Several developmental psychologists have identified the current model of urban and community living as unsuitable for people, especially for children and their parents. Under this model, the parents must bear the full responsibility of raising their children (with many being overwhelmed), as opposed to sharing that responsibility with a safe, stable, and functioning community in which families may be embedded.[37]

Children are future citizens, and their experiences growing up in a city will shape their basic behavior patterns later on. Therefore, cities that are well planned and well designed, with low-carbon and climate-resilient features, and that are planned with the participation and the perspective of children, will create future-proof sustainable patterns with correlating low-carbon behavior patterns.

The recognition of childhood as a crucial time for gaining access to the urban setting and enjoying its advantages is key to defining spatial solutions for people of all ages. Child-responsive cities have the best-practice standards for sustainable communities and cities, including compact, mixed-use places served by public transit; pedestrian-friendly environments; safe and secure pedestrian networks and public spaces; and green parks. These standards align with the principles behind healthy cities and age-friendly cities.

Cities for children. Adapting cities to the needs of children or integrating those needs into the planning of new urban communities, so that children have safe places to play and interact, will be critical in societies characterized by smaller and single-parent families (photo by UNICEF).

---

[37]   M. Montessori. 1949. *The Absorbent Mind.* Madras, India: Theosophical Publishing House; R.H. Largo. 2020. *The Right Life: Human Individuality and Its Role in Our Development, Health And Happiness.* London, United Kingdom: Penguin; Gehl Institute, Gehl (architecture and planning firm), and the Bernard van Leer Foundation. 2017. *Space to Grow: Ten Principles that Support Happy, Healthy Families in a Playful, Friendly City.* New York: Gehl Institute. Of the 10 principles, the relevant one is principle 6: Take collective responsibility for children.

Box 1: The Healthy Cities Concept

The World Health Organization (WHO) defines a healthy city as "one that is continually developing those public policies and creating those physical and social environments which enable its people to mutually support each other in carrying out all functions of life and achieving their full potential."[a]

Regarding the first WHO document on healthy cities, published in 1986, Hancock and Duhl describe 11 qualities of a healthy city as follows: (i) a clean, safe, high-quality environment; (ii) stable and sustainable ecosystem; (iii) strong, mutually supportive and nonexploitative community; (iv) public participation (life, health well-being); (v) meeting the basic needs of all people (food, water, shelter, income, safety, work); (vi) offering a variety of experiences and resources, contacts, and interactions; (vii) diverse, vital, and innovative economy; (viii) encouraging connections with cultural and biological heritage; (ix) possessing a form and design that enhances the above parameters and personal behavior; (x) public health and patient care services for all; and (xi) high positive health status and low disease status. [b]

WHO's Regional Office for Europe suggests that a city can become a healthy one if it adopts the healthy cities approach. It seeks to improve health in cities through good urban governance that puts health high on the political and social agenda. This approach recognizes the determinants of health and the need to engage all stakeholders in achieving them, supported by a set of core values, including equity, social inclusion, inter-sectoral management, and community participation. These values explicitly hold that urban health development is everyone's business.[c]

---

[a]   WHO. 1998. *Health Promotion Glossary*. Geneva.
[b]   L.J. Duhl and T. Hancock. 1988. Promoting Health in the Urban Context. *WHO Healthy Cities Papers*. No.1. Copenhagen: FADL (for the WHO Healthy Cities Project).
[c]   WHO. Health Promotion: Healthy Cities.

Source: The authors.

Box 2: The Healthy China 2030 Program

In 2016, the National Patriotic Health Campaign Committee of the People's Republic of China (PRC) defined a healthy city as an upgraded version of a hygienic city, stating that "through the improvement of urban planning, construction and management, the city improves the natural environment, social environment, and health services and popularizes healthy lifestyles to meet residents' health needs and to achieve the coordinated development of urban construction and human health." Healthy cities in the PRC focus on (i) constructing healthy environments, (ii) building a healthy society, (iii) optimizing health services, (iv) fostering healthy people, and (v) developing a health culture. The six key tasks include constructing healthy cells (healthy schools, institutions, and communities), establishing health governance models, improving environmental and sanitary infrastructure, improving safety management of drinking water, increasing environmental quality, and boosting public security systems.[a]

---

[a]   J. Yang et al. 2018. The Tsinghua-Lancet Commission on Healthy Cities in China: Unlocking the Power of Cities for a Healthy China. *Lancet*. 391 (10135). pp. 2140–2184.

Source: The authors.

ADB's Strategy 2030 aims to achieve a prosperous, inclusive, resilient, and sustainable Asia and Pacific region. It includes seven operational priorities. Improved health is implicitly related to all of the priorities, and it is an explicit objective in three of them:

(i)   **Operational priority 1: Addressing remaining poverty and reducing inequalities.** This would entail enhancing "the employability and job readiness of graduates" by supporting the achievement of better health for all, aiming for universal health coverage, strengthening social-protection systems and service delivery for those in need, and building human capital.

(ii)   **Operational priority 4: Making cities more livable.** This priority includes capacity development in planning and investments and the provision of integrated solutions to help build livable cities that are inclusive, green, competitive, and resilient. ADB will (a) pursue crosscutting projects to promote urban health, urban mobility, gender equality, and environmental sustainability; and (b) help improve urban environmental infrastructure and services contributing to health, including water supply; sanitation; wastewater and solid waste management; disaster risk reduction and climate change adaptation (reducing risks of flooding, heat waves, and storm surges, among others); and mitigation (helping to reduce emissions).

(iii) **Operational priority 7: Fostering regional cooperation and integration.** This will be achieved by promoting regional public goods; supporting mitigation of cross-border risks, including communicable and infectious diseases; and promoting regional cooperation, including on health policies, sanitary and phytosanitary standards, and quarantine policies.[38]

The HIA and HACAMP will

(i)   contribute to Strategy 2030 objectives to improve urban health, the environment, health services, and health insurance, and to respond to demographic change, meeting the needs of aging societies;

(ii)   align with and contribute to the implementation of operational priority 4, generally supporting inclusive urban development, but also supporting environmental and economic enablers and engagement;

(iii) improve the quality of urban health services and monitor their health effects on urban residents;

(iv)   encourage urban planning and design to improve health by providing appropriate transport and housing choices, reducing wastewater overflows and pollution, and improving physical and mental health;

(v)   help meet the needs created by demographic changes in a rapidly urbanizing Asia and Pacific region, in both types of developing member countries—those that are rapidly aging and those that have a growing youth population—by identifying risks, as well as opportunities to improve accessibility, health, and safety in cities for people of all ages;

---

[38]   ADB. 2018. *Strategy 2030: Achieving a Prosperous, Inclusive, Resilient, and Sustainable Asia and the Pacific.* Manila.

(vi)   contribute to the country partnership strategy for the PRC (2021–2025), with expected support for healthy and age-friendly cities; and

(vii) be adapted to and applied in other developing countries in cooperation with ADB's Sustainable Development and Climate Change Department, Economic Research and Regional Cooperation Department, and regional departments.

Healthy and age-friendly urban action examples. What follows are examples of areas of actions and opportunities to integrate healthy and age-friendly dimensions in urban planning, design, and management. These include opportunities to improve health and age-friendly outcomes by integrating urban planning and development with health and age-friendly elements, considering structural and nonstructural measures, and including planning and design features:

(i)   **safe and clean air, soil, and water (drinking and surface water); sanitation and solid waste management (including medical waste)** through better hygiene; clean, safe, and healthy urban environments; and safeguarding from respiratory and/or waterborne illnesses, and from infectious diseases associated with medical waste;

(ii)   improved accessibility to basic affordable food supplies within walking distance, with better access to **fresh, safe, and nutritious food**;

(iii) **affordable and well-designed social housing** to reduce exposure to vector-borne illnesses and communicable diseases, increase resilience to extreme heat and cold, and improve mental well-being and active community life;

(iv)   improved accessibility to **decentralized and high-quality health services**, insurance, and promotion; and social services and preventive services to allow people to actively manage their health;

(v)   **connected neighborhoods** providing improved intergenerational and gender-sensitive social interactions and well-being;

(vi)   ensured contiguous **universal accessibility** in open spaces, housing, public buildings, and public transport facilities and vehicles, to allow people to age in place and remain active in their communities and social networks;

(vii) **increased green, blue, and open spaces** (permeable) that allow physical activity, social interactions, and better mental health, but also build resilience to climate change (by mitigating urban heat island effects) and extreme weather events (heat waves) and reduce urban noise levels;

(viii) **healthy schools** with natural lighting, natural ventilation, a safe and peaceful indoor environment, nutritious food, and safe and secure pathways to and from schools and kindergartens, as well as safe drinking water, good sanitation facilities, and hygiene education that encourages the development of students' healthy behaviors throughout their lives;

(ix)   **interventions for older persons and persons with disabilities** who walk more slowly, need frequent breaks and public toilets, and need to prevent falls;

(x)   **public lighting** to ensure community safety and security;

> The recognition of childhood as a crucial time for gaining access to the urban setting and enjoying its advantages is key to defining spatial solutions for people of all ages.

(xi)   better access to **active mobility options,** including walking, cycling, and public transport, which will help achieve recommended physical activity levels, and will have multiple co-benefits such as reduced motor vehicle use, travel times, emissions, air pollution, noise, and traffic congestion;

(xii) **sponge-city green infrastructure** to reduce urban flooding, improve urban drainage, recharge groundwater, and clean storm water, while providing urban green spaces; and

(xiii) **renewable energy production** and smart grids to reduce air pollution and engage cities, communities, and people in distributed energy production systems.

3 Healthy China 2030 Program

The PRC launched the Healthy China 2030 program on 25 October 2016 (footnote 7). It is a comprehensive program that calls for adherence to the Health in All Policies (HiAP) approach to the prevention and treatment of disease and the promotion of health, healthy lifestyles, and physical fitness. The program emphasizes the importance of cities and promotes the integration of health issues into urban planning. It identifies HIA as an important mechanism for operationalization, and for the promotion of cross-sectoral collaboration and action for health. The PRC recognizes the HIA as an important tool for strengthening the organization and implementation of efforts to improve the quality of urban environments and promote and protect the health of urban residents.

The strategy builds on the related Hygienic City Campaign, which was established in 1992 to replace the Patriotic Hygiene Campaign and to reflect the spirit of reform, although the name of the organizing body remains the Patriotic Hygiene Committee to this day. The Hygienic City Campaign aims not only to clean up the public environment and educate people in the participating cities, but also to work with other major planning initiatives to transform the appearance of urban areas and promote environmental cleanliness—with such improvements as infrastructure for pollution prevention and sewage treatment. In addition to soft targets such as "visual cleanliness," the campaign sets hard targets, such as the proportion of wastewater treated or the number of public toilets per unit of population. Participating cities have to implement a range of improvements to meet the targets set by the campaign organizer in the Ministry of Health, in Beijing. In a last phase, achievements are checked by a group of inspectors who rely on both objective and subjective judgments to decide whether a city can receive the title of "Hygienic City."[39]

By adopting the HiAP approach as official policy, the Government of the People's Republic of China has put health at the center of its entire policy-making machinery. The approval of Healthy China 2030 by the Central Party Committee and the State Council, the first medium- to long-term national strategic plan for the health sector since the PRC's founding in 1949, reflects a high political commitment to participation in global health governance and to the achievement of the Sustainable Development Goals (SDGs). Inter-sectoral collaboration and action play a key role in Healthy China 2030, as many health challenges are linked to wider determinants of health that affect all health outcomes. As tackling existing and emerging health challenges within the health system and relying on health-care services alone are simply not sustainable, Healthy China 2030 focuses on prevention,

---

[39] B. Li et. al. 2015. *Motivating Intersectoral Collaboration with the Hygienic City Campaign in Jingchang, China. Environment & Urbanization.* 27 (1). pp. 285–302.

rather than treatment; on the promotion of healthy lifestyles and physical fitness; and on the development of healthy cities. The government recognizes that HIA is a useful tool for implementing the HiAP approach, and for mainstreaming inter-sectoral action for health and healthy cities.[40]

Figure 2: Relationship between Urban Health Challenges and Health Outcomes in the People's Republic of China

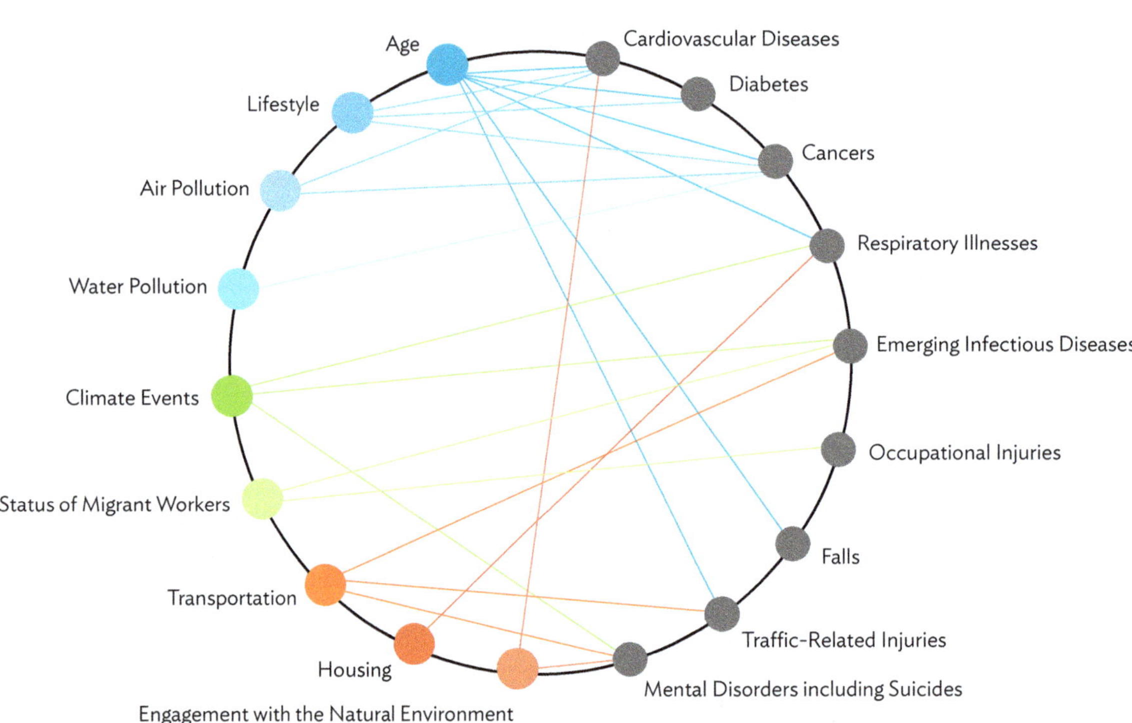

Source: The authors adapted from: J. Yang et al. 2018. The Tsinghua-Lancet Commission on Healthy Cities in China: Unlocking the Power of Cities for a Healthy China. *Lancet*. 391 (10135). pp. 2140–2184.

---

40   WHO. Healthy China 2030 (from Vision to Action); State Council, People's Republic of China. State Council Measures to Enhance People's Fitness, Health.

4 Framework and Principles for Health Impact Assessment and for Healthy and Age-Friendly City Action and Management Planning

The HIA and HACAMP framework for healthy cities is a practical and flexible approach to implementing HiAP and inter-sectoral action for healthy and four-generation-friendly cities. The health challenges confronting urban populations are complex and deeply influenced by all aspects of urban life, including the various needs of the different age groups.

As cities are dynamic systems, an HiAP and healthy and age-friendly cities approach to health improvement must not only focus on existing urban areas, urban renewal processes, and urban health challenges, but also ensure that all new urban plans and development projects are conceptualized through a health and four-generation lens. Such a dual focus will enable the embedding of healthy urban planning and healthy and universal urban design principles in new developments, while tackling existing risks and impacts in the built environment.

The scope of the application of the HIA and HACAMP framework and methods is, therefore, ambitious and comprehensive, including the following:

(i) **HIA and HACAMP for existing urban areas.** An assessment of health in existing urban areas will map out current public health challenges and identify ways to tackle them through inter-sectoral action. Retrofitting a HACAMP can bring to light the actions needed to improve or remediate existing unhealthy urban environments. As existing urban areas may face many health and aging risks that need to be mitigated, the objective is to assist city administrators and planners in identifying and prioritizing key issues and interventions, both structural and nonstructural, related to the urban environment and the apparent and emerging population health profile. A city-wide assessment could be undertaken, or a narrower geographical scope could be defined. The urban environment and related population would be characterized, and important health and aging issues identified and resolved.

(ii) **HIA and HACAMP for new urban development plans and projects.** When new urban areas or projects are planned, an HIA can be undertaken to assess their potential health implications, embed healthy urban planning elements and healthy design features, mitigate potential risk and impacts, and identify complementary interventions. City governments can fully leverage positive health outcomes from public infrastructure and private developments to maximize overall health benefits and equity.

The proposed framework builds on tested approaches to healthy urban development, such as WHO's Urban Health Equity Assessment and Response Tool (Urban HEART), which tackles existing urban health needs and challenges, and the HIA, which focuses on prospective urban developments (boxes 3 and 4). Developing healthy and age-friendly cities would benefit from a comprehensive application of this framework, which would ideally start from a city-wide health assessment of existing urban areas, followed by a systematic application to new urban developments. Given the broad scope of its application, the framework is designed with flexibility and adaptability in mind, and can be implemented to suit the needs and opportunities of different cities and of different urban-planning, policy, and project-development cycles.

Box 3: The Urban Health Equity Assessment and Response Tool

The World Health Organization (WHO) Urban Health Equity Assessment and Response Tool (Urban HEART) analyzes health issues and the unequal and potentially inequitable distribution of health care within existing urban areas and among urban populations. The tool helps to select strategies, interventions, and actions for promoting health and reducing such inequities. It considers health determinants and risk factors, and their interactions across multiple levels and sectors, as they impact various health outcomes—such as infectious diseases, noncommunicable diseases, nutrition-related disorders, psychosocial conditions, and accidents and injuries. It is inclusive enough to generate buy-in, participation, and effective dialogue among key stakeholders, but it is not sufficient as planning tool.

Source: The authors.

Box 4: The Urban Health Impact Assessment

The health impact assessment (HIA) will operationalize a Health in All Policies (HiAP) approach, and enable future inter-sectoral actions for health by focusing on newly proposed initiatives—policies, plans, programs, or projects—from every urban sector before they are implemented. The HIA will assess proposed sectoral actions while they are being planned and developed, ensuring that they consider health implications and contribute to a healthy and sustainable urban environment. The HIA will systematically use qualitative, quantitative, and participatory methods.[a] It will map out options for managing and mitigating health risks and impacts; outline monitoring, surveillance, and response mechanisms; and serve as the basis of a health management plan.[b] Industry associations strongly support HIAs,[c] which have contributed to positive returns on investments in preventative health actions.[d] Since 1992, the Asian Development Bank (ADB) has supported HIAs and provided some of the earliest HIA guidance.[e] More recently, ADB provided HIA capacity building and technical assistance in the Greater Mekong Subregion.[f] Several HIA demonstration projects have been completed across Asia and the Pacific.[g]

[a] World Health Organization (WHO). Health Impact Assessment.
[b] International Finance Corporation (IFC). 2009. Introduction to Health Impact Assessment. Washington, DC; ADB. 1992. Guidelines for the Health Impact Assessment of Development Projects. ADB Environment Papers. No. 11. Manila.
[c] Global Oil and Gas Industry Association for Environmental and Social Issues (IPIECA) and International Association of Oil & Gas Producers (IOGP). 2016. Health Impact Assessment: A Guide for the Oil and Gas Industry. London: IPIECA-IOGP Health Committee; International Council on Mining and Minerals (ICMM). 2010. Good Practice Guidance on Health Impact Assessment. London.
[d] Prevent. 2015. Return on Prevention: Benefit-Cost Analysis of Prevention Measures for Business Travelers and International Assignees. Leuven, Belgium.
[e] ADB. 1992. Guidelines for the Health Impact Assessment of Development Projects. ADB Environment Papers. No. 11. Manila.
[f] Health Impact Assessment Network: Asia Pacific.
[g] ADB. 2016. HIA: Greater Mekong Subregion Health Impact Assessment Project. Manila.

Source: The authors.

Applying a "health and four-generation lens" to urban planning and project development can help achieve multiple objectives and co-benefits, while reducing negative economic impacts from diseases in cities. The primary mission of cities should be to protect and promote the health and well-being of its citizens, as well as productivity and economic vitality. Analysis of the health implications of urban development should, therefore, be included in every city's approach to planning, governance, finance, communications, implementation, and monitoring of its own policies and projects. WHO recognizes the urban HIA as one of "the good practices for working across sectors to reduce health risks and enhance health benefits from sector-based policies."[41] See Box 4 for a description of HIAs in urban settings.

The cross-sector HIA and HACAMP framework primarily aims to provide a structured and practical approach to the assessment of health and aging needs, challenges, impacts, and opportunities of existing urban areas and of new urban developments, to inform the development of the HACAMP (Figure 3). The HACAMP should be jointly prepared and administered by city planners and public health specialists, environment specialists, and other stakeholders. It can be developed for existing urban areas (e.g., as an urban rehabilitation and retrofitting plan) or for planned new or rehabilitated areas.

The approach emphasizes the importance of urban determinants of health, and acknowledges that cities need to invest in public and community health; high-quality basic infrastructure and urban services; clean and green environments; healthy lifestyle options; disease prevention; climate resilience; high-quality health, education, and other social services; universal urban design to ensure accessibility for people of all ages and for the physically impaired; age-friendly public transport; and accessible, attractive, public green spaces. The HIA and HACAMP framework should maximize positive health outcomes. A well-prepared cross-sector HIA will effectively evaluate and propose actions for the management of health and safety risks, and serve as the basis for the development of a HACAMP, with actions and prioritized investments to enhance positive health drivers and an urban health monitoring and urban health management program.

The framework is designed for the PRC's cities and prioritizes the health and aging experiences and outcomes of urban residents—whether permanent, temporary, or with rural *hukou* (a system of household registration). City administrators are key players in implementing the framework, and in developing, applying, surveilling, and communicating the HACAMP. HIA and HACAMP outputs should be considered living documents, to be regularly reviewed, discussed, and updated; and they should help those involved in urban planning to prioritize and implement projects in an ever-evolving cityscape.

The expected impacts of mainstreaming the HIA and HACAMP include the achievement of the Healthy China 2030 vision. Expected outcomes include reduced health-care expenditures and enhanced productivity, quality of life, and well-being in greener, cleaner, and more livable cities. These cities would have public parks, be well served by public transport, and provide an attractive pedestrian and cycling environment. The framework will help prevent or manage emerging infectious diseases (and other health emergencies) better across sectors, agencies, and stakeholders.

> The primary mission of cities should be to protect and promote the health and well-being of its citizens, as well as productivity and economic vitality.

---

[41]   WHO. 2016. *Health as the Pulse of the New Urban Agenda: United Nations Conference on Housing and Sustainable Urban Development; Quito – October 2016*. Geneva.

The expected impacts of mainstreaming the HIA and HACAMP include the achievement of the Healthy China 2030 vision.

The healthy cities movement in the PRC shows that urban plans and projects can be successful with strong government leadership, availability of a mechanism for wide participation and collaboration, experience from the Hygienic City Campaign, a profound academic interest in research on the topic, and a genuine desire to seek collaboration. Projects that serve the well-being of local residents are more likely to succeed if they have the full support of local governments and health-relevant policies based on local conditions (footnote 30). These broad elements are cornerstones of the proposed framework.

Underpinning the HIA and HACAMP process is the engagement of leaders, experts, and communities. Besides political support on all levels of local government and across administrative departments, human and financial resources, capacity building, and technical assistance, the success of the HIA and HACAMP will require formal multisectoral collaboration. Establishing memorandums of understanding or similar instruments with city administrators, administrative bureau officials, and other institutions, stakeholders, and communities will be helpful in establishing a commitment to the HIA and HACAMP and in broadening support and ownership. This will ensure a lasting commitment to the approach in case of leadership change. Such memorandums of understanding will acknowledge the support and dedication of personnel, and will invite them to share their knowledge and expertise and to assist in other aspects of the preparation and implementation of the HIA and HACAMP. Senior city officials should be the main executors of the HACAMP.

Municipal leaders, administrators, and bureau officials will need to dedicate financial and human resources to establishing and supporting the HIA and HACAMP team. As urban development is dynamic, the decision-making personnel should be senior officials capable of acquiring resources and making timely decisions. Human and financial resources will be needed from other institutions and/or agencies. A dedicated staff must share information and data with the HIA and HACAMP team, participate in all phases, and help develop and implement urban planning and management measures to maximize health promotion and mitigate risks and impacts.

The framework should be applied as a step-by-step, structured, transparent process of evidence gathering, planning, and risk and action prioritization to tackle existing and future health risks associated with the physical urban pattern, urban environment, and urban governance. Cities can adapt a proposed generic process to fit local needs, taking into account the city size, development level, climate conditions, economic activities, and risk exposure. This is done with a view to mainstreaming these processes into domestic urban projects or donor-financed initiatives such as ADB's project designs, implementation, and monitoring. The process should be:

(i)   comprehensive, taking into account the health determinants for all the age groups, and of their interactions across multiple levels and sectors, and resolving the concerns of multiple sectors;

(ii)   inclusive, fostering participation and dialogue among urban stakeholders and communities, including the vulnerable;

(iii) easy to use, generating results for an intuitive understanding of urban health, aging challenges, and possible mitigating actions;

(iv) operationally feasible and sustainable, prioritizing cost-effective options for gathering data from existing information systems, and rooted in institutional mechanisms of local governments; and

(v) actionable, developing action plans that generate results and enable better governance and decision-making, emphasizing the use of forward-looking and forecasting data to identify focused interventions.

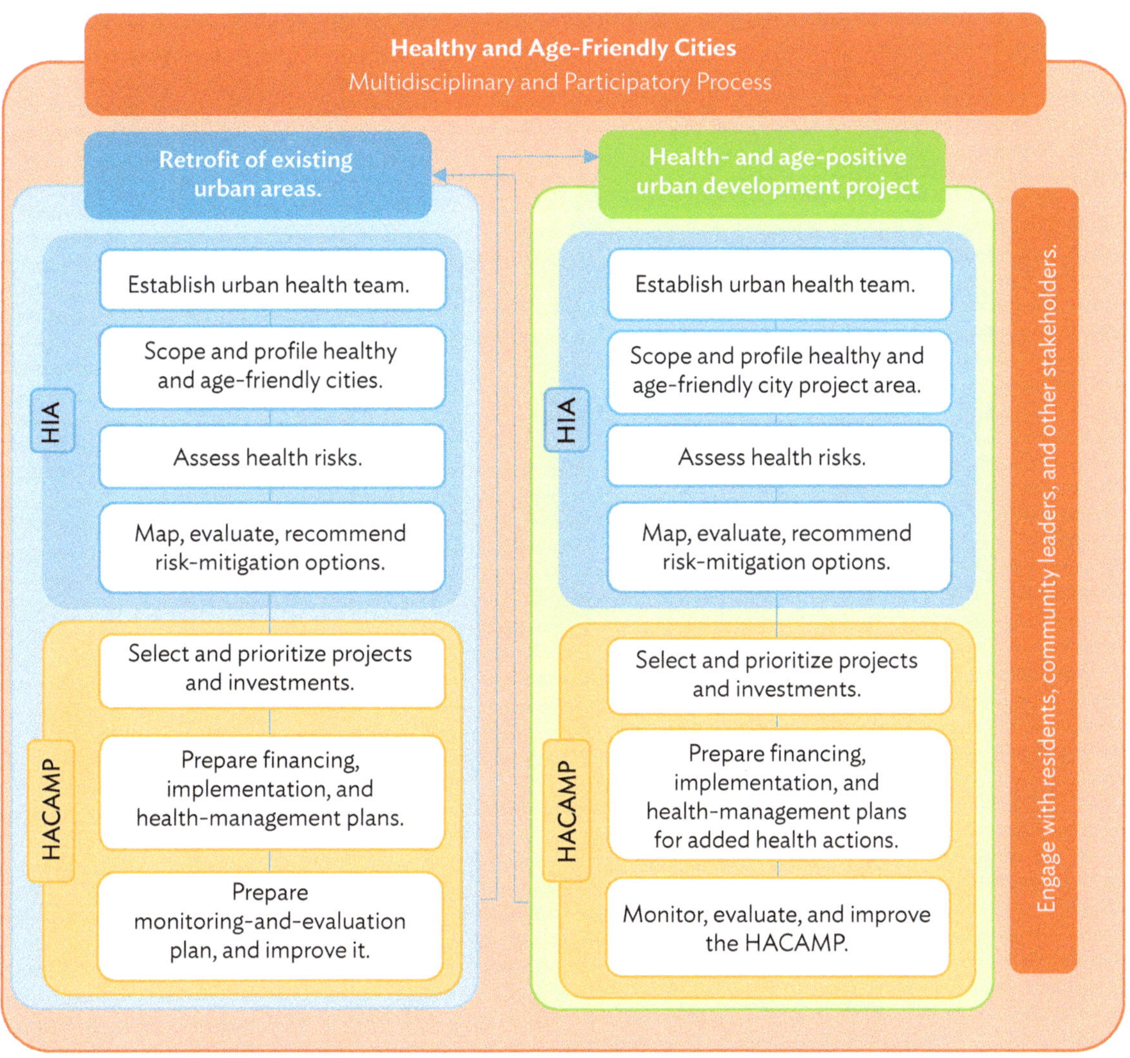
Figure 3: Health Impact Assessment and Healthy and Age-Friendly City Action and Management Plan Framework

HACAMP = healthy and age-friendly city action and management plan, HIA = health impact assessment.
Source: The authors.

Underpinning the HIA and HACAMP process is the engagement of leaders, experts, and communities.

While the assessment of existing urban areas or new master plans or projects will not be one size fits all, it will revolve around sound evidence, inter-sectoral collaboration for health, and community participation.

The use of sound evidence will be ensured by gathering reliable, transparent, and complete data that reflect health, age, and equity issues. If no data are available, alternative available data should be used or new data generated.

The framework will require inter-sectoral action and the close engagement of all relevant sectors. To influence a broad range of health determinants, collaboration will build on constructive relationships with individuals and agencies from outside the health sector: other government sectors such as education, transport, and public works; and community groups and nongovernment organizations. Sharing information and data resources is essential, so early engagement and buy-in of all stakeholders will be critical.

Community participation will be key, as it will enable residents to have a say in decisions concerning their health, and will promote the simultaneous use of community resources. Empowering communities to identify priorities using evidence, and then initiating actions to address those priorities, will ensure sustainable solutions to urban health inequities and other problems, even if government structures and leadership change. It also helps to increase understanding, participation, and education concerning healthy behavior in communities.

The HIA and HACAMP will be applied at a strategic level, allowing for the rapid identification of, and response to, critical issues in a dynamically changing environment with multiple projects proposed and implemented at any given time. Population demographics will change over time, as will the nature of health and age-related risks for all, including the elderly, children, and the physically and mentally impaired.

The following sections detail the application of the HIA and HACAMP framework to existing urban areas and to new master plans and urban development projects.

5 Health Impact Assessment and Healthy and Age-Friendly City Action and Management Plan Framework—Existing Urban Areas

Existing urban areas and their built environments exert social and physical pressures on choices and lifestyles that can be detrimental to people's health and pose health and age-related risks for people of various ages. These artificial pressures and risks can be modified, however. Figure 4 shows how city administrators, planners, and public health officials can turn risks into opportunities, positive pressures, and health and age-inclusiveness benefits in existing urban areas.

Applying the HIA and HACAMP framework to existing urban areas will enable key urban stakeholders, including local governments and communities, to better understand the determinants of health and their consequences; foster inter-sectoral collaboration in addressing the wider determinants of health; and urge government officials to make strategic decisions and prioritize actions and interventions tailored to urban health and age-inclusiveness. As shown in Figure 3, the HIA and HACAMP process can be organized as follows:

Preparing the HIA

Step 1: Establish an interdisciplinary, cross-sector urban health team.
Step 2: Carry out scoping and healthy and age-friendly city profiling.
Step 3: Assess health risks and impacts (adverse and positive), rank risks.
Step 4: Map, evaluate, and recommend risk-mitigation options.

Preparing the HACAMP

Step 5: Select and prioritize projects and investments.
Step 6: Prepare financing, implementation, and health-management plans.
Step 7: Prepare a monitoring-and-evaluation plan, and improve it.

HIA step 1: Establish an interdisciplinary, cross-sector urban health team

An interdisciplinary and cross-sector urban health team should be established under the guidance of a steering committee headed by the mayor, as the assessment requires strong coordination among urban sectors, levels of government, public and private stakeholders, and communities. The process should obtain support from many sectors, experts, and influential champions, who will raise awareness. By the end of this step, a network of agencies and individuals should be informed and ready to participate, and at least some stakeholder groups, agencies, and communities should be committed to begin sharing data. The urban health team must meet regularly, in its entirety, to make key decisions or as smaller working groups to discuss specific subjects or processes. The team will communicate with city leaders and all administrative departments and align the HIA and HACAMP with prior health-sector plans and overall urban development programs. The team will work with the city to prepare for health emergencies and climate and other disasters, for instance by readying surveillance systems and disaster-response plans. The team will also secure the budget for the HACAMP.

HIA step 2: Carry out scoping and healthy and age-friendly city profiling

Step 2a: Carry out scoping. The inter-sectoral team will define, in a structured and purposeful manner, the extent of the assessment and set the indicators to develop a healthy city profile. The geographical range must be defined. Ideally the entire city would be assessed, but this is often impracticable or highly resource intensive. Once the geographical scope is agreed on, the assessment can be further planned and undertaken. Urban health issues can be scoped rapidly and systematically using generic matrices and checklists. The scope can be refined iteratively by the inter-sectoral team with strong community input, including through digital means such as apps and websites. The assessment's topical scope should start by encompassing the full range of existing, felt, and expressed needs of urban residents, but can later be narrowed down to a few priority topics (e.g., transport or housing). The urban area of focus can be outlined, including associated facilities, transport corridors, populated areas, and other important features (e.g., waste facilities, industrial areas, hospitals, clinics, schools, green and blue spaces). When a response warrants further information and data, key informant interviews and/or focus group discussions can be held with community members and representatives of relevant agencies. Data should be geocoded and mapped where possible to visualize urban trends and identify potential hot spots or areas of concern.

Additional data may be needed to elaborate on identified health issues, such as the current status (e.g., rates of illness and disability, care needs) and drivers of health outcomes (e.g., knowledge, attitudes, practices, urban-design, and/or experience issues). Data collection must be supported by the urban health agency and include secondary data disaggregated by sex, age, and disability, if available. The available data can be supplemented by additional quantitative data from household surveys (if required) or by additional qualitative data that are collected, analyzed, and summarized in a healthy city profile.

Indicators must be selected carefully as they may greatly influence, for better or for worse, how a problem is framed and what actions are triggered as a result. Different types and levels of indicators are proposed, among them equity, inputs, outputs, outcomes, and impacts. Routine data mechanisms and existing databases must be used to select, collect, and analyze the indicators, but overreliance on routinely used indicators should be avoided, so as not to hamper the development of creative, aspirational indicators. It is also worth noting that administratively reported data often differ from perceptions reported by residents in surveys and focus groups, and from the conditions observed during field surveys. Using more than one data source can improve the quality and quantity of data and contribute to a more holistic and accurate assessment. When developing the indicator set, broad community consultation is required to identify local health and equity concerns. Team members must consult communities, decision-makers, and each other. While various sets of urban health indicators are available in the literature, the ones chosen for the healthy city profile should be purposeful and locally relevant.

With the scope and the indicator set defined, the data can be assembled, relying as much as possible on available datasets from diverse urban sectors. While new data collection may be necessary, it is often time consuming, financially burdensome, and unsustainable. An assessment of the quality and validity of the data should follow data collection. Further actions may include negotiating formal data-sharing agreements, setting up a data-sharing repository, managing the database, and conducting or commissioning new surveys.

Step 2b: Develop a healthy and age-friendly city profile. Analyzing the data to generate evidence and insights will enable stakeholders to see what urban health issues require responses. The data and evidence will be reported in a healthy city profile, which should be a live document that is regularly updated. The inter-sectoral team will compile an unranked registry of risks, impacts, and opportunities.

HIA step 3: Assess health risks and impacts (adverse and positive), rank risks

The health risks, impacts, and opportunities listed in the registry are assessed, then prioritized to ensure that future actions have the most positive effects possible. All stakeholders should participate in identifying the priority issues by assessing the evidence. Facilitating careful and deliberative discussions is critical, for example, through multi-stakeholder priority-setting workshops and meetings. Discussions with residents, service providers, and others can generate stories and explanations about the probable causes and consequences of urban health challenges. By the end of this step, stakeholders will be informed about health problems and their causes and contextual factors, and will have helped prioritize the problems. The ranking of risks, impacts, and opportunities should take special account of the modifiable aspects of the built environment and urban services to maximize opportunities for improvement. Stakeholders should identify aspirational goals against each identified risk or impact, as well as opportunities for action broadly described (to be detailed in subsequent steps). The assessment and prioritization of health risks, impacts, and opportunities will be reported and made publicly available. For more information on this, see the discussion on health risk assessments in section 7.

HIA step 4: Map, evaluate, and recommend risk-mitigation options

Possible responses must be mapped out, including structural and nonstructural options. This mapping exercise should be collaborative, just like the assessment exercise. The map should feature clear and actionable options for the governments and communities when tackling priority health issues. This step should be highly consultative, involving relevant urban sectors and communities. The development of structural and nonstructural options can draw from a menu of strategy and intervention packages using innovative methods such as futures thinking and visioning. Having the inter-sectoral HIA team, external experts, and communities brainstorm potential options can generate additional ideas. Communities should definitely provide their views on priority problems and actions. By the end of this step, a list of evidence-based options should give a broad idea of the possible responses

The nature of the interventions will depend greatly on the city, the process followed, and the issues and responses prioritized by stakeholders.

to priority health issues. The options and responses can be described in a plan outline—a working document explaining the urban health risks and opportunities and discussing the nature of each option proposed (structural versus nonstructural), giving a brief description of each response, including the expected roles and responsibilities of the stakeholders and the resource requirements for implementation.

HACAMP step 5: Select and prioritize projects and investments

The ranked risks and the evaluated long list of health-risk mitigation options developed in the previous step will be appraised and refined by the urban health team, in close collaboration with city leaders, agencies, public and private stakeholders, and communities. A set of structural and nonstructural options will then be selected to minimize adverse health risks and maximize health benefits with the available financial and human resources, along with a phased implementation plan. Projects will be selected that are technically feasible, socially responsive, and financially and economically viable based on a transparent set of criteria. Such criteria can include the likelihood of effectiveness; compliance with national priorities; responsiveness to community needs and expectations; and the availability of local or national government resources or international financing options, including climate financing vehicles, due to the co-benefits for healthy-city and climate initiatives.

HACAMP step 6: Prepare financing, implementation, and health-management plans

Detailed financing and implementation plans will be developed to establish priority actions, along with financing, investment, and implementation plans (or an urban retrofit plan) that detail each option; their objectives (which risks, impacts, and opportunities they aim to address); the responsible sectors charged with implementation (e.g., transportation bureau, parks and gardens bureau); other roles and responsibilities of stakeholders; technical feasibility; cost requirements; time lines (short, medium, or long term); alignment with government priorities; and management, monitoring, and evaluation components; among other considerations. The plans will go through rounds of public consultations. They will provide a detailed blueprint for improving the urban environment and operationalizing an inclusively designed healthy city. Larger-scale projects will then be filtered through the process described in the next step.

HACAMP step 7: Prepare a monitoring-and-evaluation plan, and improve it

A monitoring-and-evaluation plan will cover projects during and after implementation. Health and urban-planning experts and other experts and officials from the urban health team will closely supervise, guide, and advise on detailed planning and design, preparation and construction of structural projects, institutional change and capacity building, healthy city and community outreach, and on the promotion of healthy lifestyles. Regular monitoring should continue, including regular surveys on people's and communities' health improvement and updates of the healthy city profile. The HACAMP should be evaluated regularly to assess costs and benefits, identify gaps in operation or design, and to propose improvements during frequent urban-health team and steering-committee meetings.

This generic process can be adapted to local conditions and priorities. In fact, the interventions included in an outline or detailed action plan will likely vary greatly across cities. The interventions can include (i) policy proposals; (ii) proposals for various programs or plans, such as urban master plans; (iii) social-action, urban-design, infrastructure, and operational plans for water, sanitation, and solid waste management, including medical waste and other hazardous waste; (iv) the expansion of key urban services; (v) specific infrastructure upgrades; and (vi) proposed infrastructure or more targeted urban built-environment interventions or, most likely, a mix of them. The nature of the interventions will depend greatly on the city, the process followed, and the issues and responses prioritized by stakeholders.

The HIA and HACAMP should be regularly reviewed, with improvements proposed and implemented. The urban health team and steering committee should meet regularly after completing the seven steps and report progress to the mayor. Then the HIA and HACAMP should be applied to proposed urban rehabilitation plans, new urban area plans, urban projects, and even to large-scale events.

Figure 4: Health Impact Assessment and Healthy and Age-Friendly City Action and Management Plan Framework (Existing Urban Areas)

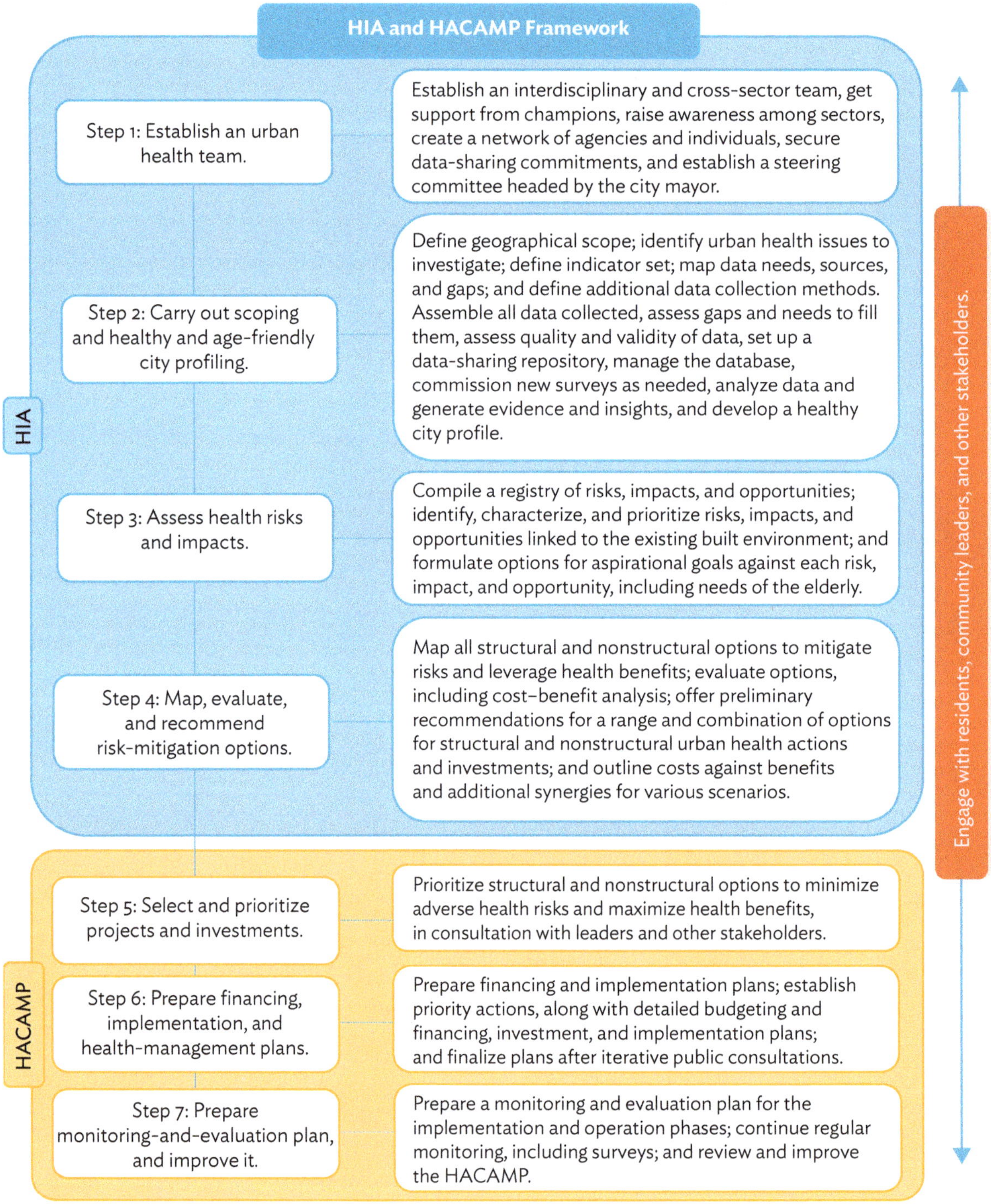

HACAMP = healthy and age-friendly city action and management plan, HIA = health impact assessment.
Source: The authors.

6 Health Impact Assessment and Healthy and Age-Friendly City Action and Management Plan Framework—New Urban Master Plans and Projects

New urban master plans and urban development projects have a tremendous influence on the health of urban residents in direct, indirect, positive, and negative ways, whether intended or not. This framework aims to assist city administrators, planners, and public health officials in assessing and health-proofing these proposals through a "health and four-generation lens," avoiding unintended health consequences and leveraging health opportunities from urban planning and development. Applied systematically to urban developments, this approach aims to ensure that cities become healthier and more age-inclusive.

The process described here is necessarily generic, given the multiplicity of possible applications. The specific scope of application for proposed future actions envisioned is not focused only on urban master plans. "Urban master plan" is used generically as an umbrella term, and the framework is intended to be applicable to other elements for development control in the hierarchy of the planning system of the PRC. These can include topic-related plans (e.g., a transport plan), district plans, detailed development control plans, or detailed construction plans, as well as urban development projects. Whatever the scope of application, the intention is to embed healthy urban planning elements and healthy design features for cities, districts, particular areas, groups of plots, specific projects, and urban services; identify complementary urban interventions; and plan for and deliver a healthier built environment.

The procedure for assessing urban master plans and projects will be a stepwise, yet iterative one. This is because decisions taken at each step will inform and enable the subsequent steps (e.g., scoping can take place only after a project has been screened), while information uncovered in later steps can feed back into previous steps (e.g., the profiling of affected communities can uncover information on additional pathways that should be scoped and included in the assessment). A generic process is proposed that can be localized by cities of varied scales and conditions, and adapted to the specific scope of application, while maintaining the same core concepts and principles. The HIA will lay out options for mitigation and leverage the positive health outcomes of a plan or project. The HACAMP will evaluate, select, and prioritize actions and investments, and will maximize positive health opportunities. It will include an implementation plan and a public health management plan to promote and protect health during the construction and operation of a policy, plan, or project.

Best practice calls for the HIA to be undertaken on prospective projects to leverage positive health outcomes from infrastructure development and to maximize health benefits. It is recommended that the HIA and HACAMP be integrated into the normal planning process of new urban development plans and projects, in order to screen for potential health implications and to systematically improve the planning and design (i.e., the land uses, urban functions, densities, public space systems, and roadway and sidewalk networks). Urban design and universal accessibility, among other factors, could have positive or negative effects on health. The HIA and HACAMP will be integrated during the planning phase to identify, plan for, and manage health risks; avoid or reduce negative, and plan for positive, impacts; and identify opportunities from the beginning. The HIA and HACAMP will also inform the economic analysis of urban infrastructure investment projects.

Once a proposal is screened and an HIA deemed required, a process similar to the one described for existing urban areas can be undertaken for new master plans and urban development projects. The HIA and HACAMP process can be organized along seven steps similar to those listed above, but with some specific assessments of the potential impacts of plans, projects, or events:

Preparing the HIA

Step 1: Establish an interdisciplinary, cross-sector urban health team.
Step 2: Carry out scoping and healthy and age-friendly city project area profiling.
Step 3: Assess health risks and impacts (adverse and positive), rank risks.
Step 4: Map, evaluate, and recommend risk-mitigation options.

Preparing the HACAMP

Step 5: Select and prioritize projects and investments.
Step 6: Prepare financing, implementation, and health-management plans for added health actions.
Step 7: Prepare a monitoring and evaluation plan, and improve it.

HIA step 1: Establish an interdisciplinary, cross-sector urban health team

Early on, an inter-sectoral HIA team should be established to steer the process and undertake the assessment (preferably with additional external, local, national, and international technical experts). The team will lead and prepare each step of the HIA and HACAMP process and meet at key decision points. Communities and public and private stakeholders should be engaged, especially during the scoping, mapping, and ranking of risks and mitigation options, and during the development of the HACAMP. The team will communicate project-related health risks and issues to city leaders and all administrative departments and align the HIA and HACAMP with urban governance and priorities.

HIA step 2: Carry out scoping and healthy and age-friendly city project area profiling

Step 2a: Carry out scoping. After the HIA team is established, scoping will identify key issues, the availability and quality of data associated with these issues, and the work plan for further HIA activities. If external technical assistance is required for undertaking the HIA, the terms of reference will be developed. The extent of the assessment will vary greatly, depending on the specific application. Scoping can benefit from various topical checklists available in the literature, and it can focus on topical plans and project typologies.

Step 2b: Develop healthy and age-friendly profile of the city project area. Profiling or baseline data collection for the plan or project area normally involves gathering existing data sets, complemented by the collection of qualitative and quantitative data to understand the contextual drivers (determinants of health) that influence health issues. If the HIA and HACAMP have already been undertaken for the proposed project location, the health city profile and underlying data collected for it can be used to develop the baseline health profile of the project-affected populations. However, the scope and scale of specific plan- or project-affected populations may require further, more spatially disaggregated data to be collected through qualitative and quantitative methods.

HIA step 3: Assess health risks and impacts (adverse and positive), rank risks

Risks and benefits will be assessed to prioritize issues and resources by reviewing contextual data related to the issues and project-related information. A health-proofing review of an urban master plan or project can ensure that the proposal is considering intended and unintended influences on health. The assessment should be a technical and participatory exercise, engaging interested and affected communities and stakeholders.

HIA step 4: Map, evaluate, and recommend risk-mitigation options

The assessment will recommend ways to improve the proposed urban master plan or project; ensure that healthy design is built into the final proposal; redesign infrastructure and introduce new processes or campaigns; and propose new infrastructure or design features to reduce disease or promote health, with an indicative budget.

HACAMP step 5: Select and prioritize projects and investments

After risks and adverse impacts are assessed and evaluated, the HACAMP will be developed by a joint team of urban planners, city government, health officials, and community representatives. For urban master plans, the joint team will review options and the indicative budget resulting from HIA recommendations based on appropriateness, feasibility, practicability, and usefulness through an urban planning lens; rank options using appropriate criteria; and consult the public on proposed interventions.

HACAMP step 6: Prepare financing, implementation, and health-management plans for added health actions

The HACAMP will be developed for final interventions, with outlined actions for each responsible urban entity and budget, and it will be integrated into the city master plan. For urban projects, the results of the health-proofing review will feed into the final project proposal to ensure that it fully integrates healthy and age-friendly urban design standards. Complementary structural and nonstructural investments will be identified to ensure that health benefits are fully leveraged and maximized.

HACAMP step 7: Prepare a monitoring-and-evaluation plan, and improve it

A management and monitoring plan will be developed to determine the usability, design, quality, and maintenance of interventions or master plan implementation. The plan will target users, including through the application of digital technologies and regular reporting to stakeholders.

The intention is to embed healthy urban planning elements and healthy design features for cities, districts, particular areas, groups of plots, specific projects, and urban services; identify complementary urban interventions; and plan for and deliver a healthier built environment.

The HIA and HACAMP can be prepared for newly planned urban areas, for entire cities, in fact. The urban health team and steering committee should remain in place to mainstream the HIA and HACAMP into all urban projects and plans.

Figure 5: Health Impact Assessment and Healthy and Age-Friendly City Action and Management Plan Framework (New Urban Master Plans and Projects)

HACAMP = healthy and age-friendly city action and management plan, HIA = health impact assessment.
Source: The authors.

7 Health Risk Assessment Tool

The HIA assesses health risks and impacts, considering the likelihood of adverse health impacts on people interacting in urban areas, spaces, facilities, and many other venues. Table 1 can serve as a basic reference.

The health risk assessment tool is derived from the ADB publication *A Health Impact Assessment Framework for Special Economic Zones in the Greater Mekong Subregion.*[42] For each health risk identified during the HIA, the level of risk is determined based on the likelihood of the event occurring and the associated consequences. There are four possible risk ratings: low, moderate, major, and catastrophic. Moderate, major, and catastrophic risks require review, attention, management, and surveillance. Low risks still require surveillance and ongoing management to ensure consistency.

Table 1: Health Risk Assessment Matrix

Level of Likelihood	Description of Likelihood	Seriousness of Medical Condition and Level of Risk				
		Minor injury or illness; first aid	Requires medical treatment; temporary impact on livelihood < 7 days	Requires medical treatment; longer-term impact on livelihood > 7 days	Prolonged major illness and/or injury; permanent impact on livelihood	Multiple cases, death, or severe injury and/or illness; permanent impact on livelihood
1	Rare—will occur only in exceptional cases or once every decade	Low	Low	Moderate	Moderate	Moderate
2	Unlikely—may occur every 5–10 years	Low	Low	Moderate	Major	Major
3	Possible—likely to happen this year	Moderate	Moderate	Major	Catastrophic	Catastrophic
4	Likely to happen monthly	Moderate	Major	Catastrophic	Catastrophic	Catastrophic
5	Expected to occur, has occurred, and has had an impact	Moderate	Major	Catastrophic	Catastrophic	Catastrophic

Source: ADB. 2018. *A Health Impact Assessment Framework for Special Economic Zones in the Greater Mekong Subregion.* Manila.

---

[42]   ADB. 2018. *A Health Impact Assessment Framework for Special Economic Zones in the Greater Mekong Subregion.* Manila.

The need to rank and prioritize health risks and to identify what actions should be taken, is illustrated in Table 2, which presents, as an example, the mitigation of traffic-related injuries and deaths.

Table 2: Example of Health Risk Management in a City: Traffic Injuries and Deaths

Description and Supporting Data	Health Consequence	Likelihood	Risk	Risk Management in Place	Management Actions	Responsibility
• Poor road conditions and driving discipline • Roads shared by multiple users in a disorganized fashion • Lack of traffic safety infrastructure, including signals, lights, stop signs, and other signage and road markings; and lack of traffic safety personnel (in case of road construction or emergencies) • Deaths and severe injuries happen weekly	5	5	Catastrophic	No	Improvement of traffic infrastructure, including the installation of safety features such as signals, signage, road markings, fences, bollards, and others, as needed	Local urban planning and transport departments, local traffic police, transport ministry
					Identification of traffic injury and mortality hot spots and analysis of causes, followed by options to reduce and manage risks to humans	Local traffic police and public health and transport ministries
					Safe driving campaigns, increased presence of traffic police and strict enforcement of traffic rules, with significant violation fees and legal action; awareness raising to effect behavior change of drivers and pedestrians	City or local authority, local police, public health ministry

Source: The authors.

8 Two Cases of ADB-Financed Projects Applying Health Impact Assessment and a Healthy and Age-Friendly City Action and Management Plan

Jilin Yanji Low-Carbon Climate-Resilient Healthy City Project, People's Republic of China

This project did a rapid HIA during its preparation phase, bringing urban health officials and urban planners together in a dialogue on healthy cities. Prior to this project, the focus of the health officials had been mainly on basic urban health issues, such as air quality, potable water, and infection prevention. The project will prepare a comprehensive HIA and HACAMP during its implementation phase. Funded by ADB, the project is located in Yanji city, which faces the challenges of poor urban livability, inadequate traffic management, exposure to climate-related flood risk, and risks to water security and safety. The project will generate multiple cross-benefits through an integrated solution provided to improve the livability of a medium-sized city. This goal is timely and essential, as there is a need to lessen migration to the coastal mega-urban regions, and the project could serve as a model for replication throughout the PRC. It will contribute to (i) the regional public goods of better health and improved air and water quality, and (ii) a revitalization of the country's economically challenged northeast. Yanji has been a pilot of the Hygienic City Campaign, so the project, including its HIAs and HACAMP, is benefiting from the technical and management experience gained during that pilot.

The project will support the first bus rapid transit (BRT) corridor in the northeast PRC, which will transform Yanji's urban geography. It will reinforce the east–west linear layout of the city by connecting key areas in a manner reflecting the principles of transit-oriented development, with higher-density, mixed-use, and pedestrian-friendly areas centered around the BRT stations. It will integrate nonmotorized transport lanes and facilities into the corridor, and will provide a series of small roads and river greenways to ensure safe and pleasant pedestrian and bicycle access to the BRT stations, while promoting low-carbon urban mobility and physical activities that enhance public health. The project-supported greenways are designed as "sponge city" green infrastructure, intended to enhance climate resilience and urban livability.[43] The project will improve the water-supply and wastewater-management systems to ensure safe and climate-resilient access to water supplies and improved water quality. Capacity development will contribute to the preparation of action plans that will showcase Yanji as a low-carbon, climate-resilient, and healthy city, contributing to the implementation of the Healthy China 2030 program and providing lessons that can be shared with other ADB developing member countries (footnote 7).

---

[43] The concept of a "sponge city" is that of a city with comprehensive urban water resource management, in which greenways, parks, and wetlands maximize ecosystem services, including storm-water management, using ecosystem-based adaptations.

The project will also address a few key challenges that directly affect human health and safety, such as congestion; traffic noise; unsafe roads; cars parked on sidewalks; water security during periods of drought; urban and river flooding; pollution of surface water during storms; poor river ecology and environments; and the lack of open spaces, especially in the urban core.

The HIA completed during the preparation phase assessed the expected health benefits of the project, such as water and air quality improvement; noise reduction; and healthier lifestyles enabled by more public transport use, walking, and cycling, and by more physical activity in general in the sponge-city open spaces and river greenways. Health benefits were predicted to be further boosted by the application of universal design principles to public spaces and facilities, especially for the benefit of women, children, the elderly, and the physically impaired. A pilot HACAMP will be prepared during project implementation to support the Healthy China 2030 program. Moreover, the project will be introducing smart-city infrastructure that utilizes high-level information and communication technology, as well as a big data platform using the Internet of Things and artificial intelligence to integrate and manage data for the investment components. The big data platform will also aim for higher levels of cross-sector integration in Yanji (including intelligent transport-system equipment, smart water metering), and it will use data to send alerts when there are unusual consumption patterns that may be related to changing health, especially for the elderly.

The health- and safety-related economic benefits from the project were quantified for some aspects, and they were projected to have a total cumulative value of over CNY6 billion by 2050. The health and age-friendly benefit streams are expected to include:

(i) reduced exposure to air pollutants and greenhouse gases (associated with risks of pulmonary and cardiovascular diseases) due to low-carbon development and increased green space and plants;

(ii) improved water supply safety and security due to improvements in the water-supply system and to saved water resources, thereby enhancing climate resilience;

(iii) reduced exposure to polluted surface water and storm water, which are associated with risks of waterborne diseases;

(iv) reduced traffic incidents due to increased safety and traffic management and to a reduction in traffic because people would be switching to the BRT, bicycles, and walking, thus reducing numbers of injuries and fatalities;

(v) the increased physical activity of BRT users, consisting of walks to and from the BRT stations, and increased general physical activity in an improved pedestrian environment that would feature sidewalks, greenways and parks, improved bike lanes, and additional small streets, creating more links that make walking and cycling more convenient—and an associated reduction of the risk of noncommunicable diseases due to enhanced pulmonary, cardiovascular, and general immune systems (which may also lessen the severity of virus infections);

(vi) reduced risk of extreme cold and heat exposure due to increased green spaces, improvements in urban microclimates (e.g., a reduction in urban heat islands), and reduced associated illnesses and fatalities from heart attack, strokes, and other causes;

(vii) improved public awareness of healthy lifestyles through campaigns featuring ads in buses and bus stations, and in parks and plazas to promote healthy lifestyles; and

(viii) strengthened institutions and developed capacity, which contribute to enhanced integrated urban health planning and management, and to enhanced sector planning in the city.

The social-inclusion benefits of the project's integration of issues relating to transport, traffic, roads, open public spaces, and the BRT are expected to include (i) improved social equity due to direct and indirect benefits; and (ii) increased mobility and accessibility, including better access to the transit system and to other public services (e.g., health care, education, and recreation), and to social connections. The improvement of public spaces, traffic safety, and accessibility through the universal design of transport and public space systems can make cities more gender- and age-inclusive and more livable for all.

The project follows state-of-the-art sustainable integrated urban planning and design principles, which already generate many health benefits. Through the HIA process, risks and further benefits were systematically conceptualized, proposed, and as much as possible included in the investment and capacity-development component of the project. The project's four main components are:

(i) **Low-carbon multimodal urban mobility, based on transit-oriented urban development.** The focus will be on planning and building of BRT line 1, the first of three planned BRT lines. The project will integrate improvements in walking and bicycling accessibility, networks, convenience, and safety, and will contribute to overall improvements in vehicle and people movement and public health.

(ii) **Climate-resilient, ecosystem-based flood risk management, drainage infrastructure, and sponge-city green infrastructure.** Green parks and linear open spaces will link BRT stations with river greenways, helping to improve environmental and human health.

(iii) **Safe and climate-resilient water supply system and wastewater management system.** Improving the safety, efficiency, and resilience of the water supply system will help reduce waterborne diseases.

(iv) **Capacity development in low-carbon, climate-resilient, and healthy city planning; urban land use; and infrastructure planning.** The project prepared a healthy and age-friendly universally accessible city action plan and a water-safety plan, and undertook an HIA scoping mission. The project team conducted field observations and meetings with city officials from key bureaus and departments, and with community representatives.

The development of the BRT line and its multimodal integration will fundamentally transform the city's urban geography by linking most of the major urban functional areas—such as the city center, commercial centers, high-density urban residential districts, Yanbian University, People's Park, major industrial parks, government centers, a high-speed rail station, and the future airport—in an east–west direction along the northern bank of the Buer Hatong River, the city's main development trajectory. The project will improve pedestrian sidewalks and pathway links, add safe pedestrian crossings and safe access for people using the BRT stations; and improve bicycle lanes and networks, bicycle parking, and public bicycle-rental

> Health benefits were predicted to be further boosted by the application of universal design principles to public spaces and facilities, especially for the benefit of women, children, the elderly, and the physically impaired.

Figure 6: Jilin Yanji Low-Carbon Climate-Resilient Healthy City Project Map

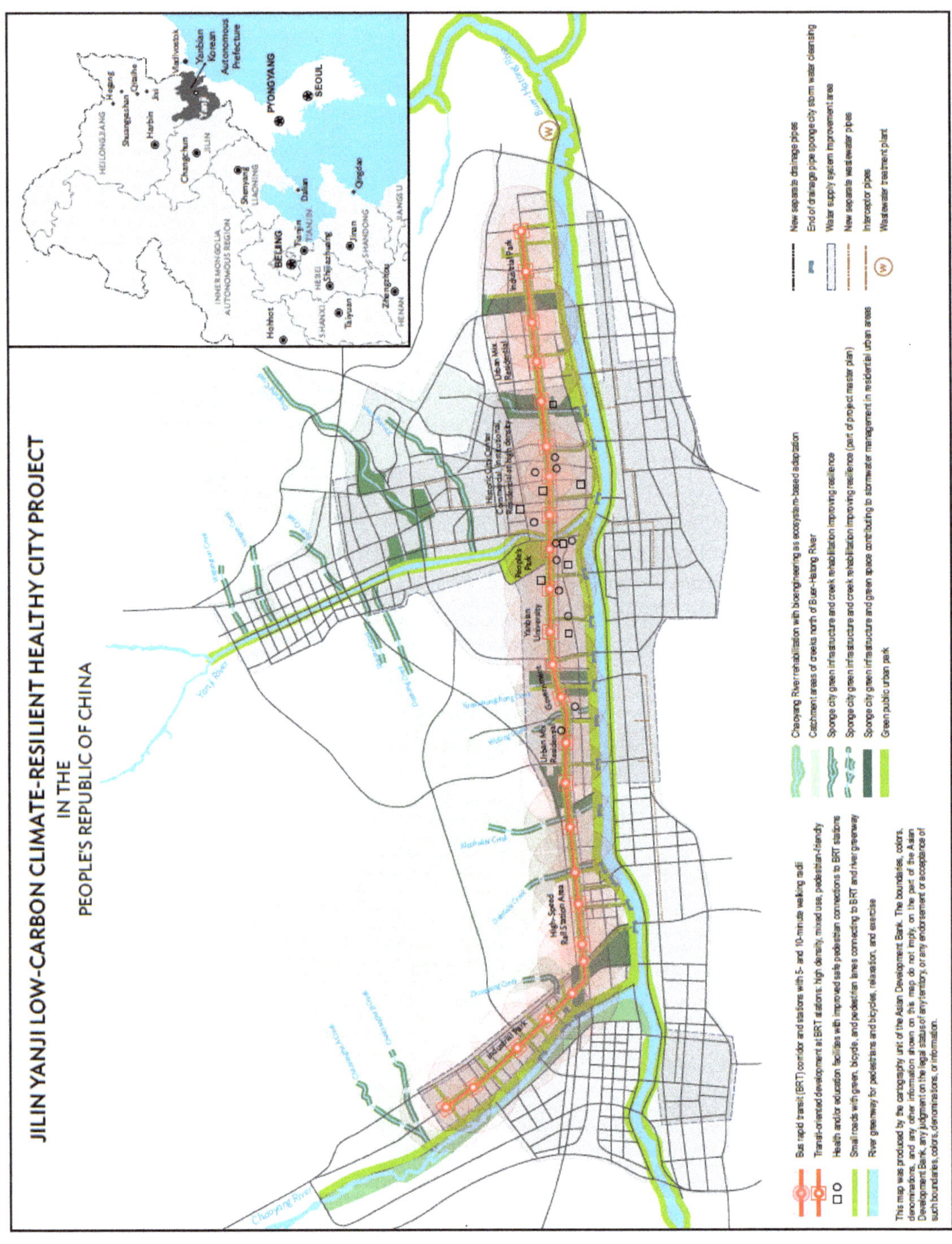

Source: Asian Development Bank.

hubs at BRT stations. The project will encourage walking and cycling, as a way to encourage healthy lifestyles. It will improve parking management, with a view to eliminating the frequent practice of parking cars on sidewalks, and will renovate sidewalk paving and landscaping, with outdoor furniture added for the safety and convenience of pedestrians. Figure 6 presents a map showing the geographic scope of the project and its expected transformative impact on the city.

International cases have proven that high-quality BRT systems that offer more comfort and convenience and faster travel times than regular bus service or private cars can induce a modal shift away from private cars, leading to short- and medium-term traffic reduction along the BRT corridor. Fewer car trips result in less fossil fuel consumption, air and noise pollution, and traffic congestion; it also results in improved traffic flow, which can, in turn, make walking and cycling more attractive, thereby improving road safety.

Transit-oriented development principles will be applied, including the preparation of station area urban development plans with compact, higher-density mixed-use districts to optimize the increased land value due to transit access. The promotion of higher-density development around stations; mixed land use (commercial, office, residential, green parks, and public facilities); urban design improvements; parking management; and improvements in the station-area access roads will maximize accessibility to public transport, promote physical activity, and limit the reliance on private cars.

A view of the future. This illustration depicts a planned bus rapid transit station in the center of Yanji city. It shows exclusive bus lanes in the middle of the avenue, rationalized and improved traffic flows, sidewalks without parked cars, safe bicycle paths, safe and attractive sidewalks and pedestrian crossings, a landscaped median and trees lining the avenue (as part of the green infrastructure), and outdoor furniture and exercise equipment (Source: Guangzhou Municipal Design Institute).

New roads promoting pedestrian and bicycle traffic are proposed in order to improve the networks for local circulation around BRT stations in selected areas that lack sufficient road links. These roads will complete the vehicular network. They will be narrower, and thus sufficient for traffic, while offering a pleasant scale for pedestrians. There will also be new narrow roads, as well as new pedestrian and bicycle paths, in industrial parks.

Pedestrian links. This boardwalk is a green and safe pedestrian path that links sponge-city green infrastructure open spaces to bus rapid transit stations (Source: Asian Development Bank).

Traffic management, road safety, and an intelligent transport system will bring improved traffic facilities and pedestrian crossings, on-street parking, and exclusive curbside bus lanes. These benefits will be reinforced through the installation of signal-control facilities; closed-circuit television; an electronic police system at selected locations; and an integrated, intelligent transport-system control center overseeing daily traffic management and operation. The system will improve traffic flow, reduce congestion and air and noise pollution, and improve road safety. And it will be integrated with parking management to discourage the use of sidewalks for vehicle parking.

Climate-resilient ecosystem-based flood risk management, drainage infrastructure, and sponge-city green infrastructure have all been utilized to rehabilitate the Chaoyang and Buer Hatong rivers, by such means as wetland rehabilitation, flood risk reduction, and improved ecosystem services. This project component will include sponge-city green infrastructure and will link BRT station areas by linear greenways, thereby allowing water-retention and infiltration areas to also serve as publicly accessible green parks, as this will enhance climate resilience; improve the urban microclimate; and sustainably reduce flood risk, especially during heavy rainfalls over the rainy season. There will also be pedestrian and bicycle paths along ecologically landscaped river greenways and linear sponge-city green infrastructure. This will give the public more access to green spaces and nature, with the associated benefits of enabling people to restore their mental health and well-being, and to engage physical activities and social interactions.

The safe and climate-resilient water supply system and wastewater management components of the project will reduce water leakage and improve management efficiency. The project will replace old and leaking water-distribution pipes, install flow meters for the district metering area, and install water meters in homes in older residential areas. The project is expected to save 4.8 million cubic meters of water annually. The wastewater and drainage component will include the construction of separate sewer and drainage pipes; these pipes

Ecological landscape of a rehabilitated river. Shown here is a river that has undergone an ecological rehabilitation, which enabled better flood-risk management and improved the river's ecological system, water infiltration capacity, and water detention and flow capacity, as well as the landscaping along the river banks contributing to more livability. A similar rehabilitation process is planned for the Chaoyang River, in Yanji city, using river-edge design principles that could also be applied to creeks in the project area (Source: Asian Development Bank).

are currently combined for wastewater and stormwater, so flooding regularly occurs during heavy downpours in the summer. Overall, the project will strengthen the city's water-supply and wastewater management; improve water quality; and reduce wastewater, flooding, and health and safety risks.

The main project components will deliver a number of positive health co-benefits and contributions, such as better air and water quality, noise reduction, and green and healthy mobility and lifestyle options. The HIA conducted during the preparation phase offered important observations and recommendations for improving the healthy and age-friendly city design, baseline assessment, and management through various actions and investments, among them the following:

(i)　the development of capacity for preparing the HIA and HACAMP;

(ii)　preparation of a water safety plan;

(iii)　consultations with the community to ensure that public spaces (especially to and from BRT stations, but also within wider station areas) are healthy, age friendly, and universally accessible, with additional features like community spaces, outdoor seating, exercise equipment, public toilets, and well-lit pathways and spaces, as well as smoke- and alcohol-free zones;

(iv)　inclusion of dementia-friendly features in BRT stations and along the routes to and from the stations, as well as on sidewalks and in other public spaces;

(v)　safe routes to schools, hospitals, elderly care facilities, urban centers, and green spaces; and

(vi)　the development of additional open green spaces in the city center.

The grand total of cumulative health-related economic benefits by 2050 is expected to be more than CNY6 billion.

Detailed health and age-friendly urban investments and activities as outcomes and outputs of the project will include:

(i)   a BRT line about 20 kilometers (km) long, with at least 25 stations, equipped with wheelchair access, alarm buttons for women, priority seating, safe lighting, and heated spaces for commuters in cold weather (especially for women)—all to make the BRT line and stations elderly- and child-friendly, and social and disability-sensitive;

(ii)   at least 30 km of pedestrian links to BRT stations, including safe crossings and routes to schools, hospitals, and elderly care facilities, following universal design principles, and with lighting to ensure safety for women, children, and the elderly;

(iii)   at least five plazas with landscaping and exercise equipment for all ages near the BRT stations;

(iv)   sidewalk parking removed in at least six locations along the BRT corridor, and 100 new parking spaces provided near BRT stations;

(v)   at least 30 km of bicycle lanes along the BRT corridor, linking to BRT stations and parking facilities at BRT stations;

(vi)   well-lit public spaces and parks that are smoke- and alcohol-free, so they may serve as child- and elderly-friendly activity areas, with exercise, dancing, and sports facilities, and children's playgrounds—to be used for free;

(vii)   at least 4 km of the river with bicycle and pedestrian paths, green embankments, and ecological low-water-level in-stream channels to lower flood risk;

(viii)   at least 8,000 square meters of sponge city stormwater-retention green space that will also serve as relaxation and recreation areas for people of all ages;

(ix)   at least 43 km of drainage pipes and 40 km of wastewater pipes, at least two end-of-storm water-pipe sedimentation tanks, and reed-bed sand filters to clean out first-flush stormwater; and

(x)   consultations; public awareness and education campaigns; and training of trainers, students, the elderly, and other stakeholders in public health, healthy low-carbon lifestyles, traffic safety, environmental protection, and safety in a four-generation urban society.

Detailed health and age-related capacity development activities and associated targets during the implementation of the project will include: (i) a detailed healthy and age-friendly city action and management plan; (ii) a public health monitoring and management program; (iii) inclusion of world-class standards in healthy and age-friendly city planning and management, utilizing information and communication technology, the Internet of Things, participatory approaches, inter-sectoral collaboration, and other features as needed; (iv) a standardized monitoring framework to assist city officials in tracking the progress of healthy city initiatives, making use of existing monitoring and review processes; and (v) the contribution of health-related data to the project and to Yanji's geographic information system base.

The project will ensure the integration of universal-design and healthy-environment principles into the planning of infrastructure. It will prepare and carry out stakeholder consultations and public awareness campaigns on public health management, healthy-city and universal-design principles, healthy lifestyles, and other themes, as needed. The project will prepare knowledge product(s), organize or help organize and/or contribute to knowledge-sharing events, to discuss lessons from demonstration, pilot, and best-practice experience in other cities of the PRC and across the Asia and Pacific region. It will also ensure the construction of a universal-design; gender-, age-, and disability-sensitive BRT, as well as safe BRT stations for all. And it will conduct capacity building campaigns for staff, including bus drivers working for the BRT, on road safety and safe driving, station operation management, emergency first aid, etc. There will also be community consultations on the needs and designs of BRT vehicles, lines, and facilities (including BRT station locations, facilities, etc.).

The many additional health benefits from the expected project outcomes were described, and some of them quantified, in an economic analysis comparing costs and benefits that was methodologically feasible and sound. According to this analysis, the grand total of cumulative health-related economic benefits by 2050 is expected to be more than CNY6 billion. Included in the calculation were the benefits from improved traffic and road safety, travel time savings, increased physical exercise due to people switching from private vehicles to the BRT, and improved air quality caused by reductions in greenhouse gas emissions. The health benefit streams from the sponge-city green infrastructure will include increased physical activity, higher air and water quality, improved microclimate, and spaces for respite. The quantified benefits will include the willingness to pay for green spaces, which will account for an accumulated economic benefit estimated at roughly CNY600 million by 2050, most of which will be directly associated with health. The cumulative total of the economic benefits from improved water-supply services is estimated to reach about CNY1 billion by 2050, some of which will also contribute to health.

Yunnan Lincang Border Economic Cooperation Zone Development Project, People's Republic of China

This project conducted a rapid HIA during project preparation, but a continuous HIA and a HACAMP are to be prepared during project implementation. The project seeks to improve infrastructure and integration facilities, regional cooperation, and local economic development in the Lincang Border Economic Cooperation Zone, in Yunnan Province. A comprehensive environmental impact assessment has been conducted for the project, which had requested a rapid HIA to (i) characterize the health conditions and issues for the people living in the project area, (ii) assess and prioritize the health risks and opportunities for workers and community members that the project may engender, and (iii) identify culturally and contextually appropriate health mitigation and enhancement measures the project should implement.

Project outputs and subprojects include a border trade market for residents, an international cooperation area, trade area roads, a bridge, water supply and wastewater treatment, municipal solid waste management, river rehabilitation, new-energy public transport facilities, a new elementary school built, and another elementary school upgraded. There will also be two new hospitals: the PRC–Myanmar Friendship Hospital, with 56,000 square meters of space and an inpatient bed capacity of 500; and a new hospital in Qingshuihe, with 9,000 square meters of space and an inpatient bed capacity of 100. Both hospitals will include maternity and obstetrics and gynecology departments. The project outcome is an expected annual increase in the ratio of medical staff per population in the economic cooperation zone by 2%, from 242 in 2017.

During the rapid HIA, a triangulation of preexisting data and primary data collected during a field mission identified (i) an increased risk of communicable disease transmission during construction and operation because of preexisting conditions and increased migration of temporary workers; (ii) increased pressure on and demand for local health services during construction by the temporary workforce; (iii) increased risk of noncommunicable diseases during construction and operation because of increased noise and shifts in livelihoods and experiences; and (iv) increased risk of traffic-related injuries during construction and operation.

The HIA team developed the following health mitigation and enhancement recommendations in partnership with local health officials:

(i)   prevent the spread of infectious diseases, and strengthen local health service capacity;

(ii)   ensure safe and healthy worker accommodations;

(iii)   support health sector relationships in the project area, and maintain low traffic injury and mortality rates;

(iv)   manage vector-borne disease risks by including built-in design measures to reduce mosquito breeding in new project areas, sites, buildings, and public spaces;

(v)   scale up and expand existing community-level health activities during construction;

(vi)   increase local health service capacity and emergency vehicles to better serve existing populations and cope with the influx of workers;

(vii)   provide occupational health services;

(viii) utilize the checklist for safe worker accommodations provided in the ADB HIA framework for special economic zones; and

(ix)   engage bilaterally with all health stakeholders to support effective and continued health-promotion and risk-prevention activities during construction.

More recommendations will be developed during implementation, in collaboration with health stakeholders in the project area, and those recommendations will inform the development of a public health management plan.

The construction phase will involve increased industrial traffic. When the economic cooperation zone is fully operational, heightened industrial traffic will become a normal part of life in the zone. Developing and implementing a traffic safety plan will be important to ensure that road traffic injuries remain low. Recommendations regarding this plan include the following:

(i)   conduct ongoing risk assessments, repeating the assessment steps of the rapid HIA at regular intervals (e.g., biannually and when there are major changes in the project design or the mix of businesses);

(ii)   assess new risks that will emerge, but could not be identified or characterized at the time of HIA preparation;

(iii) improve health surveillance and response based on health priorities; and

(iv)   assess in detail current data recording, enumeration, and analysis methods; data loss scenarios; and the process of and capacity for handling, treating, and communicating health data.

Information gathered in collaboration with project area health-surveillance professionals will help improve

(i)   health surveillance to enable accurate health data recording;

(ii) data loss scenarios to capture new cases of important communicable diseases, including mobile population cases;

(iii) the timeliness of access to health data on critical vector-, animal-, and waterborne illnesses and other communicable and infectious diseases, to ensure effective management of risks; and

(iv) coordination and collaboration on health surveillance across the border to improve data sharing on emerging risks, manage potential outbreak scenarios, and enable a focus on health opportunities.

As part of the project's capacity building on urban master planning, a health and age-proofing review of the proposed master plan designs for the economic zone areas was recommended. This will embed HACAMP principles in the master-planning process and ensure that the built environment will include enhancing features during project implementation.

9   Conclusion and Outlook

The HIA and HACAMP framework is intended to integrate, operationalize, and mainstream health and demographic-transition considerations in urban development, urban design, community planning, and project planning, and into urban management and governance. The framework aims to make health and age-friendly city planning easier for urban government officials. While the best urban-planning theories and practices do generate positive health outcomes, many existing and planned cities and urban areas still pay insufficient attention to health risks and opportunities, thus hindering their ability to produce positive health and age-friendly outcomes. The placement of health and well-being at the center of urban development and management objectives is timely and urgent, as it is needed to prepare for the emerging four-generation urban society, which will have more elderly people and fewer children, and it is timely for the current COVID-19 pandemic and afterward.

In 2018, the Tsinghua–Lancet Commission on Healthy Cities in China provided a robust and comprehensive analysis of urban health challenges specific to the PRC. The commission called for a greater inclusion of health in all policies, with a focus on urban planning; increased participation by all actors in health management (community residents, private and public sectors, and institutions and organizations); promotion of inter-sectoral action and collaboration to ensure that health is considered in a variety of contexts; the setting of local goals and assessment of progress with defined indicators; and improvements in research and education, with postsecondary institutions and the private sector supporting new and practical ways to achieve healthy urban environments (footnote 30). Applying the practical step-by-step HIA and HACAMP framework can support all these goals.

As the preparation of the HIA and HACAMP is a new process in the PRC (and in many other countries), successful implementation will require capacity building to ensure that all those involved in urban planning and management understand the core concepts and goals and the steps required for HIA and HACAMP work. Technical assistance to support management in this task will be required during the early stages of the framework's application.

The technical assistance should ensure that all team members understand the unique focus of this type of HIA, and are able to prioritize health and age-related risks to maximize benefits for urban residents. The technical assistance should fully support the team members during the first round of HIA and HACAMP activities to ensure that the process is positive, collaborative, and successful. The COVID-19 pandemic, which started in an urban context, reflects the need to take health investments in cities seriously and to take a holistic approach that considers health determinants and infectious and noncommunicable diseases. The causal relationship between COVID-19 fatality and pre-morbidity, gender, and age show how important it is to consider demographic health preconditions when managing urban health, and how important enabling healthy lifestyles and well-being in cities is. Investments in health care alone, especially in large hospital complexes, is not sufficient. A strategic, decentralized, cross-sectoral public health promotion approach is needed.

As the PRC keeps urbanizing and aging rapidly, a considerable public health shift from treatment to primary prevention and health promotion is not only a wise move, but also a necessary one. Managing the health risks of the urban built environment and leveraging the many health opportunities it provides will not only help achieve public health goals, it will also promote urban development that will improve the quality of life and prosperity in the cities. This framework aims to comprehensively contribute to leveraging these health and urban development co-benefits, and to fulfill key policy requirements of the Healthy China 2030 agenda. Experiences in the PRC will provide important lessons for other countries, including other ADB developing member countries.

The placement of health and well-being at the center of urban development and management objectives is timely and urgent.

A list of options and checklists for mitigating health risks and improving health outcomes are presented in Table A.1; a checklist of age-friendly cities from the World Health Organization (WHO) guidance document is presented in Table A.2; and a matrix showing planning principles for child-responsive urban planning and design, added from the United Nations Children's Fund (UNICEF) guidance document, is presented in Table A.3. These documents are intended to help urban planners and city administrators understand the evidence-based health benefits associated with healthy, age-friendly, and child-friendly urban planning and design features, as well as the health benefits associated with healthy, age-friendly, and child-friendly urban management, public communication, and awareness raising. The tables show overlaps, with some co-benefits applicable to all three objectives. They also show that many features are aligned with current and internationally agreed best practices for urban planning and design, and urban management and governance. The lists are not strictly in the order of priority, but they generally follow the hierarchy of needs conceptualized by the authors, who will be updating the lists as they prioritize the issues. The lists are intended for use as menus of options that should be prioritized during an HIA.[44]

Table A.1: Matrix of Urban Planning and Design Features with Positive Health Outcomes

Implementation Efforts and Modifiable Features	Specific Features and Evidence of Health Outcomes
Topic 1. Eliminating or Minimizing Exposure to Environmental Hazards, and Providing Basic Urban Services	
Improve air quality; reduce exposure to air pollution; ensure access for all to safe and secure drinking water; ensure clean surface water; ensure access to sanitation and wastewater management; ensure proper solid waste management, including hazardous waste management (also medical waste); reduce excessive noise; reduce risk of flooding.	• Ensure clean air; clean water (access to safe drinking water, sanitation and hygiene, clean surface water and groundwater); clean soil; acceptable noise levels; and protection from and/or preparedness and management of natural disasters. • Improved air quality is associated with increased physical activity among older adults. • Exposure to air pollutants has an adverse effect on many health outcomes across all population groups (increased risk of developing respiratory infectious diseases and chronic conditions, e.g., chronic obstructive pulmonary disease and type 2 diabetes, neonatal complications and poor birth outcomes, cancer, worsened respiratory outcomes and childhood mortality, among others. • Exposure to excessive noise is associated with poorer mental health outcomes, particularly among older adults and children, and it is linked to higher anxiety levels among adults. • Flooding can affect people's physical and mental health, with affected communities reporting higher symptoms of stress, mental illness, and increased risk of chronic disease.

[44]   WHO. 2007. *Global Age-Friendly Cities: A Guide.* Geneva.

Topic 2. Ensuring and Improving Community Food Infrastructure	
Promote urban food cultivation, increase provision of and access to allotments and adequate garden spaces.	• Ensure safe and easy access to affordable basic food supply within a short walking distance of each urban household. • Urban agriculture—defined as community gardens, urban farming, and farmers' markets—improves attitudes toward healthier food, increases opportunities for physical activity and social connectivity, and increases fruit and vegetable consumption. • Gardening in an allotment setting may result in numerous positive physical and mental health-related impacts and outcomes.
Topic 3. Providing Healthy, Affordable Food for the General Population	
Increase access to healthier food for the general population, decrease exposure to unhealthy food environments, increase access to healthier food in schools, and increase access to retail outlets selling healthier food.	• Access to healthy, affordable food for the general population (e.g., food in schools, neighborhood retail provision) is associated with improved attitudes toward healthy eating and healthier food purchasing behavior. • Improved dietary behaviors, such as increased fruit and vegetable consumption, are associated with increased access to healthy, affordable fruits and vegetables. • Increased access to unhealthy food retail outlets is associated with increased weight status in the general population, and increased obesity and unhealthy eating behaviors among children residing in low-income areas. • Provision of healthy, affordable food in schools is associated with improved healthier food sales, dietary behaviors, and nutritional outcomes. • Multicomponent interventions and an integrated, whole-school approach are both effective in improving children's diet and food choices at school. • Increased access to retail outlets selling healthier food is associated with improvements in dietary behaviors and adult weight status. • Exposure to takeaway food outlets increases consumption of takeaway food, particularly around the workplace.
Topic 4. Expanding the Stock of Affordable Social Housing for Groups with Specific Needs	
Provide affordable housing for specific vulnerable groups, people living with chronic conditions, and the homeless.	• The provision of affordable housing for vulnerable groups (including adults with intellectual disabilities and adult substance abusers) can lead to improvements in social, behavioral, and health-related outcomes. • The availability of secure and affordable housing for those with some chronic medical conditions, such as HIV/AIDS, can increase engagement with health-care services, which has been shown to improve health-related outcomes. • Access to secure and affordable housing reduces engagement in risky health-related behaviors. • The provision of affordable housing for the homeless increases their engagement with health-care services, improves their quality of life, increases employment, and improves mental health.
Topic 5. Increasing the Stock of Affordable and Diverse Social Housing	
Provide diverse housing types—mixed use, affordable, affordable rental.	• A diverse mix of housing types has been associated with increased physical activity. • The combination of mixed land use and affordable housing is strongly associated with improved perceived safety in the neighborhood, particularly among individuals from low-income groups.

Topic 6. Improving the Quality of Housing

<table>
<tr><td>Provide energy-efficient homes, remove physical hazards in homes, refurbish or retrofit housing, ensure housing has daylight and ventilation.</td><td><ul><li>Living in a warm and energy-efficient property can improve general health outcomes, reduce respiratory conditions, improve mental health, and reduce mortality.</li><li>Retrofitting modifications to improve home heating and energy efficiency may help reduce health inequalities among those from low-income groups, notably older adults and those living with chronic preexisting conditions.</li><li>Good-quality housing can reduce the risk of unintentional injury or death. For example, improvements in residential lighting and interventions to reduce hazards in the home can lead to improved social outcomes and reduce fall-related injuries among older adults.</li><li>Housing refurbishment, including damp proofing, re-roofing, and new window installation, is associated with improvements in general health outcomes and reduced health inequalities.</li><li>Energy poverty is associated with excess winter deaths, increased prevalence of chronic health conditions, and poorer mental health outcomes.</li><li>The linkages between poor indoor air quality and ill health, particularly cardiovascular diseases, respiratory symptoms, sensory irritation, lung cancer, and other cancers, are well established.</li><li>Ventilation can help control air contaminants and humidity, thereby improving indoor air quality.</li></ul></td></tr>
</table>

Topic 7. Adaptation to Climate Change Risks and Disaster Risk Management

<table>
<tr><td>Encourage neighborhood tree planting and increase urban green and blue spaces, increase (or prevent reduction of) soil permeability, address climate change, manage disaster risks, and prepare response plans and mechanisms.</td><td><ul><li>Greening (planting of trees) has a cooling effect on the environment, with an urban park being about 1°C cooler than a nongreen site.</li><li>The implementation of green infrastructure may reduce the effects of the urban heat island.</li><li>Stagnant weather can reduce air quality and negatively affect health by trapping warm and cold air, leading to smog.</li><li>Green-space and public-open-space strategies need to be planned in accordance with the climate and irrigation needs; they can be adapted to climatic and environmental changes, such as drought.</li><li>Disaster risk management governance, systems, mechanisms, and budgets should be in place to minimize the impacts of disasters on human health, safety, and security.</li></ul></td></tr>
</table>

Topic 8. Improving Connectivity and Traffic Safety

<table>
<tr><td>Improve street connectivity and public realm (e.g., providing street lighting).</td><td><ul><li>Enhancing street connectivity by providing walking and cycling infrastructure, and by improving access to public transportation, can help reduce perceptions of long-distance trips and provide alternative routes for active travel.</li><li>Public realm improvements such as the provision of street lighting in residential areas can prevent road traffic collisions and increase pedestrian activity.</li><li>General environmental improvements have the potential to reduce fear of crime.</li></ul></td></tr>
</table>

Topic 9. Travel and Road Safety	
Prioritize pedestrians and cyclists, implement traffic-calming measures, and improve the public realm.	• Efforts to prioritize pedestrians and cyclists through changes in physical infrastructure (e.g., separation of cycling and pedestrian infrastructure from road traffic) are associated with positive behavioral and health outcomes and encourage active travel. • Traffic-calming measures, including speed humps, speed tables, cushions, and roundabouts, increase the tendency to walk and reduce risk of pedestrian injury. • Traffic-calming measures are effective when used in 20-mile-per-hour (mph) zones. • Home zones, which can reduce traffic speed to 10–15 mph, reduce the risk of road traffic collisions. • Public realm improvements, such as street lighting, have been shown to increase physical activity among older adults and to reduce road traffic.
Topic 10. Public Transport	
Encourage the use of public transport.	• Combining public transport with other forms of active travel, such as walking and cycling, can improve cardiovascular fitness. • The provision of high-quality public transport is associated with higher levels of active travel among children. • Active travel in areas with low pollution levels is associated with increased physical activity among older adults. The perception of air pollution appears to constitute a barrier to participation in outdoor physical activity and active travel. • Affordable public transportation helps alleviate social isolation.
Topic 11. Mobility and Accessibility for All Ages and Activities: Universal Design	
Improve access to recreational spaces, promote active travel to work and school.	• The application of universal design principles to all public spaces—such as sidewalks, plazas, parks, public buildings and facilities, and transport systems—will create a pleasant, safe, and secure environment for walking for everyone, including vulnerable people such as children, the elderly, and the physically and mentally impaired. • Built-environment strategies to promote physical activity can have a positive impact on engagement in physical activities. For example, better access to playgrounds and recreational facilities is associated with increased walking among adolescents. • Active travel to school or work leads to improved cardiovascular. • Resolving mobility issues among the mentally and physically impaired can improve their quality of life.

Topic 12. Enhancing Neighborhood Walkability	
Increase neighborhood walkability and improve infrastructure to support walking and cycling.	• Improved street connectivity, mixed land use, and compact residential design are important features of a walkable neighborhood. • Improving neighborhood walkability and access to recreational and non-recreational destinations (grocery stores, schools, and other amenities) can encourage active travel and have a positive impact on social interaction among older adults. • Investing in infrastructure to support walking can increase levels of physical activity among all age groups. • The availability of outdoor seating is a necessary urban feature for older people, as many of them have difficulty walking around their neighborhoods without somewhere to rest. • The condition of sidewalks has an obvious impact on the ability to walk around a neighborhood. Sidewalks that are narrow, uneven, cracked, or congested, or that have high curbs or obstructions, present potential hazards and affect the ability of older people to walk around. The following features are often recommended as ways to make sidewalks age-friendly: a smooth, level, nonslip surface; and sufficient width to accommodate wheelchairs. • Other age-friendly features are dropped curbs that taper off to be level with the road; clearance from obstructions such as street vendors, parked cars, and trees; and priority access for pedestrians. • Universal access encourages older people to be more active.
Topic 13. Building Complete and Compact Neighborhoods	
Build compact neighborhoods, and increase access to facilities and amenities.	• Compact neighborhoods (those with higher street connectivity, typically designed with finer grid patterns) with diverse land-use mixes and greater residential densities are generally more conducive to nonmotorized transport. • Long distances to recreational facilities, steep inclines, and increased proximity to amenities have been identified as having a negative impact on walking and cycling. • The provision of local amenities can improve mobility and social engagement among older adults. Mixed land use developments that prioritize access to schools, recreational centers, and social amenities can increase physical activity among children, adolescents, and older adults.

Topic 14. Access to and Engagement with the Natural Environment	
Provide access to, and opportunities to engage in, the natural environment; and make parks more attractive.	• Access to and engagement with the natural environment is associated with improved physical and mental health, and with a reduced risk of mortality and of chronic conditions such as cardiovascular disease. • Access to recreational facilities, such as parks and playgrounds, is associated with a reduced risk of obesity among adolescents and an increase in physical activity. • Living close to green spaces such as parks can improve health, regardless of social class. • Improving the appearance of parks can increase their use and encourage physical activity among children and older adults. • Physical activity in a natural setting is associated with better mental-health outcomes than physical activity indoors. • People value public open green spaces for reasons that vary with age, culture, and socioeconomic status. This spectrum of values and activities must be considered when planning public open green spaces. To achieve best-practice public open-space and green-space planning, planners must identify the needs of the current and predicted future community. Participation by the community in the planning and design of green spaces is an important step toward understanding these needs. Engagement not only encourages community ownership of the open space, but may also maximize its use. • In addition to a focus on the number and size of public open spaces in a community, greater consideration should be given to the quality and maintenance of those spaces, as evidence shows that they are important for physical and mental health. Good-quality green spaces shaped by public open-space strategies should include trees, gardens, walking paths, grassed areas, amenities, dog-related facilities and off-leash areas, water features, and wildlife. For biodiversity, good-quality open spaces should include a variety of habitats, structurally complex understory vegetation, and specific habitat features such as tree hollows. Threatened species and ecological communities should be preserved and supported.
Topic 15. Active Travel Infrastructure	
Increase infrastructure for walking and cycling.	• Investing in infrastructure to support walking can increase physical activity levels and improve mobility among children, adults, and older adults. • Prioritizing active travel by investing in cycling infrastructure can lead to improved cardiovascular outcomes and improved weight status among children, adults, and older adults.

mph = miles per hour.

Sources: E. Bird et al. 2017. *Healthy People Healthy Places Evidence Tool: Evidence and Practical Linkage for Design, Planning and Health.* Technical Report. Bristol: University of the West of England; M. Davern et al. 2017. *Quality Green Space Supporting Health, Wellbeing and Biodiversity: A Literature Review.* Report prepared for the National Heart Foundation of Australia (South Australian Division); Government of South Australia, Department of Environment, Water and Natural Resources and the Office for Recreation and Sport; South Australian Local Government Association; and the University of Melbourne. Adelaide: The National Heart Foundation of Australia (South Australian Division).

Table A.2: Matrix of Age-Friendly Urban Planning and Design Features

Topic 1. Age-Friendly Outdoor Spaces and Buildings Checklist	
Environment	The city is clean, with enforced regulations limiting noise levels and unpleasant or harmful odors in public places.
Green spaces and walkways	• There are well maintained and safe green spaces, with adequate shelter, toilet facilities, and seating that can be easily accessed. • Pedestrian-friendly walkways are free from obstructions, have smooth surfaces, have public toilets, and can be easily accessed.
Outdoor seating	Outdoor seating is available, particularly in parks, transport stops, and other public spaces, and they are placed at regular intervals; the seating is well maintained and patrolled to ensure safe access by all.
Sidewalks	• Sidewalks are well maintained, smooth, level, nonslip, and wide enough to accommodate wheelchairs, with low curbs that taper off to the level of the road. • Sidewalks are clear of any obstructions (e.g., street vendors, parked cars, dog droppings, snow), and pedestrians have priority of use.
Roads	• Roads have adequate nonslip, regularly spaced pedestrian crossings, enabling pedestrians to cross safely. • Roads have well-designed and appropriately placed physical structures, such as traffic islands, overpasses, or underpasses, to help pedestrians cross busy roads. • Pedestrian crossing lights allow sufficient time for older people to cross roads, with the aid of both visual and audio signals.
Traffic	There is strict enforcement of traffic rules and regulations, with drivers giving way to pedestrians.
Bicycle paths	There are separate paths for cyclists.
Safety	Public safety in all open spaces and buildings is a priority and is promoted by, for example, measures to reduce the risk from natural disasters, good street lighting, police patrols, enforcement of bylaws, and support for community and personal safety initiatives.
Services	• Services are clustered, and located in close proximity to where older people live, so they can be easily accessed (e.g., on the ground floor of buildings). • There are special customer-service arrangements for older people, such as separate queues or service counters.
Buildings	Buildings are accessible and have the following features: elevators, ramps, adequate signage, railings on stairways, stairs that are not too high or steep, nonslip floors, rest areas with comfortable chairs, and sufficient numbers of public toilets.
Public toilets	Public toilets are clean, well maintained, easily accessible for people with varying abilities, well signed, and placed in convenient locations.
Topic 2: Age-Friendly Transportation Checklist	
Affordability	• Public transportation is affordable to all older people. • Consistent and well-displayed transportation rates are charged.
Reliability and frequency	Public transport is reliable and frequent (including services at night and on the weekends).
Travel destinations	• Public transport is available to take older people to key destinations such as hospitals, health centers, public parks, shopping centers, banks, and seniors centers. • All areas are well-serviced with adequate, well-connected transport routes within the city (including the outer areas) and between neighboring cities. • Transport routes are well-connected between the various transport options.

Age-friendly vehicles	• Vehicles are accessible, with floors that lower, low steps, and wide and high seats. • Vehicles are clean and well maintained. • Vehicles have clear signage indicating the vehicle number and destination.
Specialized services	Sufficient specialized transport services are available for people with disabilities.
Priority seating	• Priority seating for older people is provided, and is respected by other passengers.
Transport drivers	• Drivers are courteous, obey traffic rules; stop at designated transport stops; wait for passengers to be seated before driving off; and park alongside the curb, so that it is easier for older people to exit the vehicle.
Safety and comfort	Public transport is crime-free and not overcrowded.
Transport stops and stations	• Designated transport stops are located close to where older people live, have seating and are sheltered from inclement weather, are clean and safe, and are adequately lit. • Stations are accessible, with ramps, escalators, elevators, appropriate platforms, public toilets, and legible and well-placed signage. • Transport stops and stations are easy to access and are conveniently located. • Station staff are courteous and helpful.
Information	• Information is provided to older people on how to use public transport and on the range of transport options available. • Timetables are legible and easy to access. • Timetables clearly indicate the routes of buses accessible to disabled people.
Community transport	Community transport services, including volunteer drivers and shuttle services, are available for taking older people to specific events and places.
Taxis	• Taxis are affordable, with discounts or subsidized taxi fares provided for older people with low incomes. • Taxis are comfortable and accessible, with room for wheelchairs and/or walkers. • Taxi drivers are courteous and helpful.
Roads	• Roads are well maintained, wide, and well lit. They have appropriately designed and placed traffic-calming devices; traffic signals and lights at intersections; clearly marked intersections; covered drains; and consistent, clearly visible, and well-placed signage. • The traffic flow is well regulated. • Roads are free of obstructions that might block a driver's vision. • The rules of the road are strictly enforced and drivers are educated to follow the rules.
Driving competence	Refresher driving courses are provided and promoted.
Parking	• Affordable parking is available. • Priority parking bays are provided for older people close to buildings and transport stops. • Priority parking bays for disabled people are provided close to buildings and transport stops, the use of which is monitored. • Drop-off and pickup bays close to buildings and transport stops are provided for handicapped and older people.
Topic 3: Age-Friendly Housing Checklist	
Affordability	Affordable housing is available for all older people.
Essential services	Essential services are provided that are affordable to all.

Design	• Housing is built out of appropriate materials and is well structured.
	• There is sufficient space to enable older people to move around freely.
	• Housing is appropriately equipped to meet environmental conditions (e.g., appropriate air-conditioning or heating).
	• Housing is adapted to the needs of older people, with even surfaces; passages wide enough for wheelchairs; and appropriately designed bathrooms, toilets, and kitchens.
Modifications	• Housing is modified for older people as needed.
	• Housing modifications are affordable.
	• Equipment for housing modifications is readily available.
	• Financial assistance is provided for home modifications.
	• There is a good understanding of how housing can be modified to meet the needs of older people.
Maintenance	• Maintenance services are affordable for older people.
	• There are appropriately qualified and reliable service providers to undertake maintenance work.
	• Public housing, rented accommodations, and common areas are well maintained.
Aging in place	• Housing is located close to services and facilities.
	• Affordable services are provided to enable older people to remain at home, to "age in place."
	• Older people are well informed about the services available to them, to help them age in place.
Community integration	Housing design facilitates continued integration of older people into the community.
Housing options	• A range of appropriate and affordable housing options is available for older people, including frail and disabled older people, in the local area.
	• Older people are well informed about the available housing options.
	• Sufficient and affordable housing designed for older people is provided in the local area.
	• There is a range of appropriate services, amenities, and activities in older people's housing facilities.
	• Older people's housing is integrated into the surrounding community.
Living environment	• Housing is not overcrowded.
	• Older people are comfortable in their homes.
	• Housing is not located in areas prone to natural disasters.
	• Older people feel safe in the environment they live in.
	• Financial assistance is provided for housing security measures.
Topic 4: Age-Friendly Social Participation Checklist	
Accessibility of events and activities	• Senior centers are conveniently located, with affordable, flexible transportation available.
	• Older people have the option of participating with a friend or caregiver.
	• The timing of events is convenient for older people during the day.
	• Admission to events is open to all (i.e., no membership required), and purchasing a ticket is a quick, one-stop process that does not require older people to queue up for a long time.

Affordability	• Events, activities, and local attractions are affordable for older participants, with no hidden or additional costs (such as transportation costs). • Voluntary organizations are supported by the public and private sectors to keep the costs of activities for older people affordable.
Range of events and activities	• A wide variety of activities is available to appeal to a diverse population of older people, each of whom may have many interests. • Community activities encourage the participation of people of different ages and cultural backgrounds.
Facilities and settings	• Gatherings that include older people occur in a variety of community locations, such as recreation centers, schools, libraries, community centers in residential neighborhoods, parks, and gardens. • Facilities are accessible and equipped to enable participation by people with disabilities or by those who require care.
Promotion and awareness of activities	Activities and events are well advertised to older people, including information about each activity, its accessibility, and transportation options.
Addressing isolation	• Personal invitations are sent to promote activities and encourage participation. • Events are easy to attend, and no special skills (including literacy) are required. • A club member who no longer attends events is kept on the club's mailing and telephone lists unless the member asks to be taken off. • Organizations make an effort to engage isolated seniors through, for example, personal visits or telephone calls.
Fostering community integration	• Community facilities promote shared and multipurpose use by people of different ages and interests, and they foster interaction among user groups. • Local gathering places and activities promote familiarity and exchange among neighborhood residents.
Topic 5: Age-Friendly Respect and Social Inclusion Checklist	
Respectful and inclusive services	• Older people are consulted by public, voluntary, and commercial services on ways to serve them better. • Public and commercial organizations provide services and products adapted to older people's needs and preferences. • Services have helpful and courteous staff trained to respond to older people.
Public images of aging	The media include older people in public imagery, depicting them positively and without stereotypes.
Intergenerational and family interactions	• Community-wide settings, activities, and events attract people of all ages by accommodating age-specific needs and preferences. • Older people are specifically included in community activities for families. • Activities that bring generations together for mutual enjoyment and enrichment are regularly held.
Public education	• Learning about aging and older people is included in primary and secondary school curricula. • Older people are actively and regularly involved in local school activities with children and teachers. • Older people are provided opportunities to share their knowledge, histories, and expertise with other generations.

Community inclusion	• Older people are included as full partners in community decision-making affecting them. • Older people are recognized by the community for their past as well as their present contributions. • Community action to strengthen neighborhood ties and support include older residents as key advisers, actors, and beneficiaries.
Economic inclusion	Economically disadvantaged older people enjoy access to public, voluntary, and private services and events.

Topic 6: Age-Friendly Civic Participation and Employment Checklist

Volunteering options	• There is a range of volunteering opportunities for older people. • Voluntary organizations are well developed, with infrastructure, training programs, and a workforce of volunteers. • The skills and interests of volunteers are matched to positions (e.g., via a register or database). • Volunteers are supported in their work, for example, by being provided with transportation or having the cost of parking reimbursed.
Employment options	• Policy and legislation prevent discrimination on the basis of age. • Retirement is a choice, not an obligation. • There are flexible opportunities, with options for part-time or seasonal employment for older people. • There are employment programs and agencies for older workers. • Employee organizations (e.g., trade unions) support flexible options, such as part-time and volunteer work, to enable more participation by older workers. • Employers are encouraged to employ and retain older workers.
Training	• Training for post-retirement job opportunities is provided for older workers. • Retraining opportunities, such as training in new technologies, is available to older workers. • Voluntary organizations provide training for their positions.
Accessibility	• Opportunities for voluntary or paid work are known and promoted. • Transportation to work is available. • Workplaces are adapted to meet the needs of disabled people. • There is no cost to the worker for participating in paid or voluntary work. • There is support for organizations (e.g., funding or reduced insurance costs) to recruit, train, and retain older volunteers.
Civic participation	• Advisory councils, boards of organizations, etc. include older people. • Support exists for enabling older people and people with disabilities to participate in meetings and civic events by providing, for instance, reserved seating, aids for the hard of hearing, and transportation. • Policies, programs, and plans for older people include contributions from older people. • Older people are encouraged to participate in civic activities.
Valued contributions	• Older people are respected and acknowledged for their contributions. • Employers and organizations are sensitive to the needs of older workers. • The benefits of employing older workers are explained to employers.

Entrepreneurship	• There is support for older entrepreneurs, and for offering them opportunities for self-employment (e.g., markets for selling farm produce and crafts, small-business training, and microfinancing for older workers). • Information designed to support small and home-based businesses is presented in a format suitable for older workers.
Pay	• Older workers are fairly remunerated for their work. • Volunteers are reimbursed for the expenses they incur while working. • Older workers' earnings are not deducted from their pensions and other forms of income support to which they are entitled.
Topic 7: Age-Friendly Communications and Information Checklist	
Information dissemination	• A basic, universal communications system of written and broadcast media and telephone reaches every resident. • Regular and reliable distribution of information is ensured by the government or voluntary organizations. • Information is disseminated to older people close to their homes and where they conduct their usual activities of daily life. • Information dissemination is coordinated by an accessible community service that is well-publicized—a "one-stop" information center. • Regular information and program broadcasts of interest to older people are offered in both mainstream and targeted media.
Oral communications	• Oral communications accessible to older people are preferred, for instance through public meetings, community centers, clubs, and the broadcast media, and through individuals responsible for spreading the word one to one. • People at risk of social isolation get information from trusted individuals with whom they may interact, such as volunteer callers and visitors, home support workers, hairdressers, doormen, or caretakers. • Individuals in public offices and businesses provide friendly, person-to-person service on request.
Printed information	Printed information—including official forms, television captions, and text on visual displays—has large lettering, and the main ideas are shown by clear headings and bold-face type.
Plain language	Print and spoken communications use simple, familiar words in short, straightforward sentences.
Automated communications and equipment	• Telephone answering services give instructions slowly and clearly, and tell callers how they can repeat the message at any time. • Users have the choice of speaking to a real person or of leaving a message for someone to call back. • Electronic equipment, such as mobile phones, radios, televisions, and bank and ticket machines, has large buttons and big lettering. • The display panel of bank, postal, and other service machines is well-illuminated and can be seen by people of different heights.
Computers and the internet	• There is wide public access to computers and the internet, at no or minimal charge, in public places such as government offices, community centers, and libraries. • Tailored instructions and individual assistance for users are readily available.

Topic 8: Age-Friendly Community and Health Services Checklist	
Service accessibility	• Health and social services are well-distributed throughout the city, are conveniently co-located, and can be reached readily by all means of transportation. • Residential care facilities, such as retirement homes and nursing homes, are located close to services and residential areas, so that residents can remain integrated into the larger community. • Service facilities are safely constructed and are fully accessible for people with disabilities. • Clear and accessible information is provided about the health and social services for older people. • Delivery of individual services is coordinated, with a minimum of bureaucracy. • Administrative and service personnel treat older people with respect and sensitivity. • Economic barriers impeding access to health and community support services are minimal. • There is adequate access to burial sites.
Available services	• An adequate range of health and community support services is offered for promoting, maintaining, and restoring health. • Home-care services on offer include health services, personal care, and housekeeping. • Health and social services address the needs and concerns of older people. Service professionals have appropriate skills and training to communicate with and effectively serve older people.
Voluntary support	Volunteers of all ages are encouraged to assist older people in a wide range of health and community settings, and are given support for these activities.
Emergency planning and care	Emergency planning includes older people, taking into account their needs and capacities when preparing for and responding to emergencies.

Source: World Health Organization (WHO). 2007. *Global Age-Friendly Cities: A Guide*. Geneva.

Table A.3: Principles of Child-Responsive Urban Planning and Design

The Importance of Focusing on Children	
The central role for urban planning in achieving the Sustainable Development Goals, from a global perspective to a local context, is creating thriving and equitable cities where children live in healthy, safe, inclusive, green, and prosperous communities. Analysis of the main urban areas shows that urbanization does not necessarily induce sustainable urban environments for children. Cities are drivers of prosperity, but also of inequity. Although mostly overlooked, inequity has a spatial dimension that makes children vulnerable. An unsustainable built environment has diminishing returns on service delivery for children, or even worse, makes it impossible. But the built environment can be a realm of opportunity, with planners and governments committed supporting children's rights and equity. UNICEF's 10 Children's Rights and Urban Planning Principles are based on the recognition that cities should not only support children's development, but thrive as homes for future generations.	
Principle 1: Investments	Respect children's rights and invest in child-responsive urban planning that ensures a safe and clean environment for children and involves children's participation in area-based interventions, stakeholder engagement, and evidence-based decision-making, securing children's health, safety, citizenship, environmental sustainability, and prosperity, from early childhood to adolescent life.
Principle 2: Housing and land tenure	Provide affordable and adequate housing and secure land tenure for children and the community, where they feel safe and secure, to live, to sleep, to play, and to learn.
Principle 3: Public amenities	Provide infrastructure for health, educational, and social services for children and the community, which they have access to, to thrive and to develop life skills.
Principle 4: Public spaces	Provide safe and inclusive public and green spaces for children and the community, where they can meet and engage in outdoor activities.
Principle 5: Transportation systems	Develop active transportation and public transit systems and ensure independent mobility for children and the community, so they have equal and safe access to all services and opportunities in their city.
Principle 6: Integrated water and sanitation management systems	Develop safely managed water and sanitation services and ensure an Integrated Urban Water Management system for children and the community, so they have adequate and equitable access to safe and affordable water, sanitation, and hygiene.
Principle 7: Food systems	Develop a food system with farms, markets, and vendors, so children and the community have permanent access to healthy, affordable, and sustainably produced food and nutrition.
Principle 8: Waste cycle systems	Develop a zero-waste system and ensure sustainable resource management, so children and the community can thrive in a safe and clean environment.
Principle 9: Energy networks	Integrate clean energy networks and ensure reliable access to power, so children and the community have access to all urban services day and night.
Principle 10: Data and ICT networks	Integrate data and ICT networks and ensure digital connectivity for children and the community to universally accessible, affordable, safe, and reliable information and communication.

ICT = information and communication technology, UNICEF = United Nations Children's Fund.

Source: UNICEF. 2018. *Shaping Urbanization for Children: A Handbook on Child-Responsive Urban Planning.* New York. p. 5.